Sarnoff, Jane.
    Take warning : A book of superstitions /
by Jane Sarnoff and Reynold Ruffins. New
York : Scribner, c1978.
    159 p. : ill. ; 24 cm.

    Explains superstitions concerning a wide
variety of phenomena from different times
and places.
    ISBN: 0-684-15550-8.

    1.Superstition - Dictionaries. 2.Folk-
lore - Dictionaries. I.Ruffins, Reynold.
II.Title.
                                77-26295

TAKE WARNING!
A BOOK OF SUPERSTITIONS

Dedicated to
Terry Rothchild
and to the memory of
Octavia Jeter Crispin
With special thanks to
Mina Barker

TAKE WARNING!

*A Book
of Superstitions
By
Jane Sarnoff
and
Reynold Ruffins*

CHARLES SCRIBNER'S SONS NEW YORK

Text copyright © 1978 Jane Sarnoff
Illustrations copyright © 1978 Reynold Ruffins

Library of Congress Cataloging in Publication Data
Sarnoff, Jane.   Take Warning!
SUMMARY: Explains superstitions concerning a wide variety of phenomena
from different times and places.
1. Superstition   2. Folk-lore
1. [1. Superstition.   2. Folklore]   I. Ruffins, Reynold.   II. Title.
GR81. S27   398′.41   77-26295   ISBN 0-684-15550-8

1 3 5 7 9 11 13 15 17 19 V/C 20 18 16 14 12 10 8 6 4 2

Printed in the United States of America

Red sky at night,
Sailors' delight.
Red sky in the morning,
Sailors take warning.

Sailors, scientists, and firefighters, people in cities, deserts, farms, and space capsules—everybody, everywhere, is superstitious in some way. We all want to be able to foretell the future, control the world around us, capture a thing called luck. And we become more superstitious in times of danger and calamity, or in situations where chance seems to be an important factor.

Some superstitions are beliefs (*White specks on fingernails mean good fortune*); some are practices (*Touch blue and your wish will come true*). Some are personal, some are shared by a great many people. There are even some superstitions that are known, in slightly different form, almost everywhere in the world. These basic superstitions are about things which are especially important to people—food, weather, marriage, health, and, of course, love. Then too, one person's religion is another person's superstition.

Sometimes superstitions are related. In *Take Warning!*, related superstitions are cross-referenced with a note suggesting that you see other entries. You should also see other entries for additional information about a superstition when you see words in small capital letters.

Superstitions are among the oldest—and the most universal—forms of human thought. They are also fun and interesting to read. *Take Warning!* has superstitions about almost everything and explanations about how many superstitions came to be. Do superstitions really work? Of course not. But, well . . . washing the car does seem to bring rain.

Abracadabra • The word "abracadabra," written or spoken, is a CHARM against sickness that goes as far back in time as the second century A.D. Although there are many explanations for the word, it is most likely the NAME of an ancient demon or god—probably one of the names of the sun-god Mithras. People once believed that if the name of the spirit who caused trouble was discovered and said aloud in a particular way, the power of the spirit would be stopped. Others believed that if the spirits were called on in special ways, they would have to do the bidding of the caller.

The abracadabra charm is thought to be especially helpful against toothache, infection, and fever. To stop already existing problems, the word should be said over and over, each time dropping the first syllable until only "ra" is left. When "ra" is said, the sickness will start to disappear just the way the word did. This type of charm is used with many words. In the Middle Ages in Europe special words were to be said, with a syllable or letter dropped each time, for almost every type of illness.

To prevent illness, "abracadabra" should be written, as shown here, on a piece of material. The material should then be sewn into a bag and worn around the neck on a string as an AMULET. The TRIANGLE formed by the written word helps to strengthen the charm. Triangles of this type, using abracadabra or other charms, are called "magic triangles." (See MAGIC SQUARE, SQUARE OF SATURN)

Abracadabra
racadabra
cadabra
dabra
ra

Acorn • *An acorn should be carried to bring good luck and to ensure a long life.*

Superstitions about acorns seem to exist wherever OAK TREES and acorns do. The Romans used the acorn as a symbol of fruitfulness and long life because the tall oak grew from the little acorn and lived for such a long time. The Druids, priests of an ancient religion in what is now England, thought that oak trees and acorns were sacred. To honor them would bring good luck, to harm them would bring bad luck.

• *An acorn at the window will keep lightning out.*

In ancient Scandinavia, it was believed that lightning could only enter a house through a window, and that the god Thor controlled thunder and lightning. Since Thor was known to be very fond of oak trees, an acorn was hung near a window to ask Thor to spare the house when he sent down lightning bolts. Today acorns are often used as ornaments at the end of window shade cords.

Albatross • *To kill an albatross is to bring ill luck to the ship and all upon it.*

The albatross is the largest of the seabirds which follow ships out to sea. It is often the last bird left flying with the ship, the final tie to shore. Sailors have watched albatrosses closely, thought about them often, and turned these thoughts into stories and superstitions. Some say that each albatross is the soul of a drowned sailor who follows the ship to be close to his mates. Other stories tell of an albatross, which is very strong, lifting shipwrecked sailors out of the sea and carrying them safely to shore. Certainly, it would be bad luck to kill a bird that had the soul of a shipmate or that might save your life.

Amber • *Amber beads, worn as a necklace, can protect against illness or cure colds.*

Amulet • An amulet is an object that protects against evil or brings good luck. Most often, amulets are worn to protect the wearer. They may also protect possessions and may be nailed to the door of a house, placed on a post in a field, or fastened to an automobile or bicycle. They can be RINGS, STONES, special or HOLY BOOKS, shirts, or belts—anything that is thought by the owner to have special power. Some amulets are found objects, others are purchased or blessed by a person thought to have special power. Stones with holes through them are common personal amulets throughout the world. HORSESHOES are often used as household or barn amulets. Amulets made from parts of animals are thought to give the wearer the luck and the power of the animal. A fox's tail might be hung from a bicycle to give it speed, a lion's tooth carried to give courage, a tiger skin or bear claw worn to give strength.

9

Animals • *Animals can talk while the midnight bells ring in Christmas.*

• *A dead animal should be buried near the roots of a fruit tree when the tree is planted or there will be no fruit.*
This superstition is English, but many peoples have superstitions that make it necessary to sacrifice an animal in order to ensure a good crop. The superstitions may come from fact, since growth might be particularly good near where the animal was buried. The body of the animal would serve as fertilizer for the tree or plant. There are superstitions about many animals, including the CAT, HORSE, and WOLF.

• *A china reproduction of an animal, kept in the house as an ornament, should face into the room, never toward the door.*
It was thought that the luck of the house would follow the eyes of the animal.
(See AMULET, BUYING)

Ants • *Destroying an anthill will bring bad luck.*

• *Ants become busiest when bad weather is near.*

Apple • Peel an apple all around, making one long piece of peel. Throw the skin over your LEFT shoulder and the initials of your future mate's name will appear in the twists of the peel. While throwing the apple, say the following CHARM:

> *Apple peel, apple peel, twist then rest,*
> *Show me the one that I'll love best.*
> *Apple peel over my shoulder fly,*
> *Show me the one I'll love till I die.*

• Take an apple by the stem and twist the apple while you say the alphabet. The letter you are saying when the stem breaks is the initial of your true love's first name. You can start saying the alphabet at either end.

- To choose between two lovers, take two apple seeds, name one for each lover, SPIT on the seeds and stick them on your forehead. The seed that stays on the longest shows who is the right lover for you.
- Take the seeds of an apple and name them for your lovers. Throw them one by one into a fire. The seed that makes the loudest noise indicates your true love.

- *To eat an apple without rubbing it first is to challenge the devil.* ━

- *He who plants an apple tree*
  Will live to see its end.
  He who plants a pear tree
  May plant it for a friend.

- *An apple a day*
  Keeps the doctor away.

- To find out your fate in love, count the seeds of an apple, saying:

  > *One, I love,*
  > *Two, I love,*
  > THREE, *I love, I say,*
  > *Four, I love with all my heart,*
  > *And five, I cast away.*
  > *Six, he loves,*
  > SEVEN, *she loves,*
  > *Eight, they both love.*
  > NINE, *he comes,*
  > *Ten, he tarries,*
  > *Eleven, he courts,*
  > *Twelve, he marries.*
  > THIRTEEN *wishes,*
  > *Fourteen kisses,*
  > *All the rest, little witches.*

Applesauce • *A bad woman can't make good applesauce.*
Applesauce made by a bad woman will always be mushy.

Asthma • *To cure asthma, collect spiders' webs, roll them into a ball between the palms of your hands, and swallow the ball.*

• *To cure asthma, eat carrots at every meal.*

• *To cure asthma, put the head of a live young frog into the mouth of the sufferer for a minute and the illness will pass to the frog.*

• *Asthma can be prevented or cured by sticking the tanned skin of a mole to the patient's chest with honey.*
Although this is an old English cure, one much like it has been used in parts of west Africa. A ferret skin was worn around the neck of a person with asthma, or one whose parents had asthma, to cure or prevent the illness.

Baby • *If you let a baby see itself in a* MIRROR *before it is six months old, it will become sick or die before the year is up.*
• *If you cut a baby's nails before it is a year old, it will be a thief when it grows up.*
This superstition is still kept in some parts of England. The baby's nails are bitten off rather than cut. (See EYE-LASHES, FINGERNAILS, HAIR, SPIT)
(See BIRTH, CHILDREN, TICKLE, WIND)

Bachelor's button • A small BLUE flower called a bachelor's button has been thought in many parts of the world—Asia, England, and the United States—to be able to tell if a marriage would be happy or sad. A young man in love would pick a flower early in the morning, put it in his pocket, and not look at it for twenty-four hours. If at the end of that time the bachelor's button was still fresh and blue, the marriage would be happy.

Back
• *Sew your* CLOTHES *on your back. From that time on,* MONEY *you will lack.*
(See CRACK)

Bad luck • Bad luck can be driven away if you hold the back of your right hand to your face and SPIT THREE times through the forefinger and middle finger. (See V SIGN) Another good way of warding off bad luck is to make the FIG SIGN. Many superstitions, in all parts of the world, deal with what guards against, or invites, bad luck. Although superstitions may talk about CHRISTMAS or CROWS, at their most basic, all superstitions are about good and bad luck.
(See LUCK)

At the time of death, your soul leaves your body in the shape of a raven.

Banana • *Cut a slice from the stalk end of a banana while making a wish. If there is a Y-shaped mark, the wish will come true.*

Baseball • *To* SPIT *on your hands before you pick up a baseball bat brings good luck.*
• *A baseball player who changes bats after two strikes have been called will be struck out.*
• *A piece of chewing gum stuck on the top of a baseball cap brings good luck to the team.*
• *To* CROSS *bats on a baseball field will bring bad luck to the batter.*
(See GOLF)

Basketball • *A basketball player who makes the last basket during warm-ups will do well during the game.*
• *A basketball player who makes the last basket during warm-ups will do badly during the game.*
(See GOLF)

Bat • *The heart of a bat—dried, powdered, and carried in a front pocket—will turn a bullet or stop a man from bleeding to death.*
• *If you wash your face with the blood of a bat you will be able to see in the dark.*

Bed • *If* THREE *people help to make a bed, one will become sick within a year.*
• *You must get out of bed on the same side that you get in on or you will have bad luck.*
• *Changing a bed or sweeping out the bedroom before a guest has been gone for an hour will bring bad luck to a friend of the family.*

Bed wetting • *Bed wetting can be cured by eating half of a roasted mouse.*
(See DANDELION, FIRE)

Bees • *Bee stings are a cure for rheumatism.*

• *If a member of the family dies in a place where bees are kept for honey, the bees must be told of the death or they will go away.*

Superstitions about telling bees of death—or in some places marriages, births, and other important events— are common wherever bees are kept. There is a wide- spread belief that bees are the souls of departed people and that they are in close contact with spirits and gods. (See DREAM, NEWS)

• *A bee can't sting you while you are holding your breath.* (See CHRISTMAS EVE)

Bells • Bells have often been used as AMULETS. Their sound was supposed to frighten off evil spirits. Bells have often been attached to the harnesses of camels, horses, and oxen to protect the animals, their loads, or the people driving or riding them. Bells are particularly necessary on trips into foreign lands where there might be many strange or evil spirits.

Birds • Many people have thought that birds are mes- sengers of the dead or the spirits. Birds are often thought to carry messages from the "other world" to people. The Old Testament and the Koran, the holy book of the Moslems, have passages about birds talking to man about God's will, and the Christians often sym- bolize one member of the Trinity as a dove. Indians in Brazil believed that the soul took the shape of a bird and that dreaming of a bird meant that the soul had been out of the body. The ancient Greeks thought that at death a person's soul left the body in the shape of a raven. (See SEA GULL)

• In parts of England it is thought that whatever you are doing when you hear the first cuckoo each year you will do often during the coming year. This superstition is believed in other parts of the world, but the type of bird changes from place to place. In some places the direction of the call of the bird is also important:

> *From the north, for tragedy,*
> *From the south, good crops.*
> *From the west, good luck will be,*
> *From the east, good love.*

- There are superstitions about many different birds; ROBINS, CROWS, and WRENS are a few. The importance of each bird differs from place to place, but almost everywhere, birds are thought to be special.

Birth • *Someone born at midnight has the power to see ghosts.*
- *To ensure good luck, a newborn child must be carried to the top of the house before being taken downstairs for the first time.* If the house has no stairs, even climbing with the child on top of a box or chair will help.
- *When a birth takes place when the* MOON *is on the increase, the next child born to the mother will be of the same sex.*
- *Monday's child is fair of face;*
  Tuesday's child is full of grace;
  Wednesday's child is full of woe;
  Thursday's child has far to go.
  Friday's child is loving and giving;
  Saturday's child works hard for its living.
  But the child that is born on the Sabbath day
  is fair and wise, good and gay.
- *An axe or knife under the bed will cut the pain of childbirth.*
  (See DOOR, FEET, STARS, THREE, TREE)

Birthday cake • *If you blow out all the* CANDLES *on your birthday cake with the first puff you will get your wish.*
  (See HOLY BOOKS)

Birthstone • It has long been believed that each month or sign of the ZODIAC is associated with a precious stone. Wearing your birthstone will bring you luck and pass to you the special qualities of the stone. If you own your birthstone and do not wear it, you will have particularly bad luck. Most birthstones can be worn by anyone wishing to gain their special benefits. But you should wear the stone for June or October only if you were born in that month. The stone associated with each month and the qualities attributed to it have changed throughout history. The ones given here are common in modern times.

Month	Stone	Special qualities
January	Garnet	Faithfulness; repels flying insects
February	Amethyst	Calmness; protects against drunkenness and foolish love
March	Aquamarine	Wisdom, success, and popularity
April	DIAMOND	Innocence; ensures victory over one's enemies
May	EMERALD	Love and prosperity; protects against eye disease
June	PEARL	Good luck, health, and wisdom
July	Ruby	Love; heals wounds, prevents stomachaches
August	Peridot	Contentment and personal satisfaction
September	Sapphire	Charm; protects against the EVIL EYE, relieves headaches
October	OPAL	Good fortune in all one's endeavors
November	Topaz	Friendship; guards against calamity
December	Turquoise	Prosperity; protects against accidents

Blackberries • *If you pick blackberries after the second Saturday in October, you will suffer a grave misfortune.* On the second Saturday in October the devil SPITS on blackberries and to eat one after that would be asking for trouble.

Black cat • *To see a black CAT cross your path is bad luck.* (United States)

• *To see a black cat walk toward you is good luck.* (England)

• *If the cat of your house is black,*
  Of lovers you will have no lack.

• *It is good luck if a strange black cat visits a home, but bad luck if it decides to stay.*

• In Egypt, black cats were thought to be sacred; in England, a black cat in the house could save a sailor from danger at sea and black cats in general were lucky to have around. In Germany, France, and parts of the United States, black cats were thought to be companions of witches and therefore very bad luck. If you believe that black cats are bad luck, the way to stop trouble if the black cat crosses your path is to take your hat off, turn it around on your head, and walk NINE steps before turning it around again.

Blackheads • *To get rid of blackheads, crawl* THREE *times through a* BRAMBLE ARCH *on your hands and knees in the direction that the* SUN *goes.*

Bleeding heart plant • *A bleeding heart plant in the house will bring bad luck unless a coin is placed in the soil around it.*

Blood • If lovers have quarreled and separated, one may get the other back by pricking a finger until blood comes. The blood should be used to write the initials of both people on a piece of wood. THREE CIRCLES of blood should then be drawn around the initials, and the piece of wood buried. The lovers will be together again within three days. Blood, as one of the essential body fluids, is often used in CHARMS. (See BODY, CUTS, SPIT)

Blue • *To protect yourself from witches, wear a blue bead around your neck.*
Witches do not like the color blue, it is thought, because blue is supposed to be the color of heaven. (See BRIDE, EVIL EYE, RED)

• *Wear beads of blue,*
 Keep danger far from you.
• *Touch blue*
 And your wish
 Will come true.

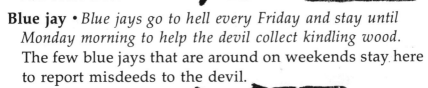

Blue jay • *Blue jays go to hell every Friday and stay until Monday morning to help the devil collect kindling wood.* The few blue jays that are around on weekends stay here to report misdeeds to the devil.

Body • *To carry a dead body on a ship is to send the winds away.*
• *To find the body of a person who has been drowned, put a loaf of bread in the water.*
The loaf will float to a spot just above the body and then stay still. (See CORPSE, DROWNING, SEVEN)

- Bodies, and the ground in which they are buried, are often thought to be connected with cures for diseases. Shrines at which believers pray for health are sometimes built near the place where a famous person is buried. The touch of a dead person, bits of bone, pieces of material on which BLOOD has fallen, dirt from a grave, or even just the act of walking around a grave, is said to cure everything from arthritis to warts.

Boils • To cure boils, pick up a STONE without looking at it, SPIT on the stone, and make a CIRCLE in the saliva, saying:

> *What I see shall increase,*
> *What I rub shall decrease.*

Then rub the stone on the boil and the boil will disappear within a week. You must carry out the cure when the MOON is getting smaller. If you do it when the moon is on the increase, the boil will get larger instead of smaller.

Book • *If you drop a schoolbook you must kiss it as you pick it up or you will forget everything you have read in it.*

Bramble arch • In parts of England, whooping cough has been said to be cured by passing a sick child through a bramble arch SEVEN times, saying:

> *In bramble, out cough*
> *Here I leave the whooping cough*

The bramble arch cure is known in many countries throughout Europe. Brambles were trained into an arch and made to take root at both ends. Rheumatism, HEADACHE, and other illnesses were thought to be cured by crawling or being passed through the arch. In other parts of the world, similar cures were carried out with arches made of other plants or by passing the sick person through the crotch of a TREE. (See IRON)

Bread • *A loaf of bread should never be turned upside down after a slice has been cut from it.*

In parts of England, the United States, and Germany, it is said that if you turn the loaf upside down you will bring bad luck to the next grain harvest. In Italy the superstition says that if you turn a loaf upside down, whether or not a slice has been cut from it, "you put God on His face."

• *If a girl pricks baking bread with a knife She will never make a happy wife.*

(See BODY, GOOD FRIDAY)

Bread and butter • If two friends are walking side by side and let a tree or other tall object come between them, they will have a serious quarrel. To break the curse, they must say at once and together, "Bread and butter." Some people say that they should hook the little fingers of their right hands as they say it.

Break • The expression "lucky break" comes from a superstition about avoiding bad luck. A primitive person who was frightened and thought that an evil spirit was nearby would break a twig or small branch, making a loud NOISE in hope that the spirit would be frightened away. If the person stopped being frightened, and his or her luck was then good, the break was said to have been a lucky break. In some parts of the world people snap their fingers at talk of trouble or to scare away a bad thought. (See KNOCK ON WOOD)

Bride

- *Something old,*
  Something new,
  Something borrowed,
  Something BLUE,
  And a lucky sixpence
  In her SHOE.

  If the bride does not wear each of the things named in this rhyme, her marriage will be a bad one.
  (See WEDDING DRESS)

- *If the bride does not cry the first time she is kissed by her husband after the wedding, she will have tears all her married life.*
- *The bride should never walk across her new doorstep the first time she enters the house as a married woman. She should be carried over by her husband.*

  This superstition goes back to the days when men took their brides by force and carried them away to their new homes. The Romans continued the idea of carrying the bride over the doorstep but did it to stop her from tripping, a bad omen, or from entering on her LEFT foot, which would bring bad luck. (See FEET) In some parts of the world it is the husband who should not walk across the doorstep and who is carried by his friends.
  (See MIRROR, ORANGE BLOSSOMS, WEDDING COUPLE)

❈

Bridge • *If you say goodby to a friend on a bridge, you will never see each other again,*
- *If you make a wish at one end of a bridge and then hold your breath and keep your eyes closed until you reach the other side, you will get your wish.*
- *If you drive under a bridge that a train is passing over, put your right hand to the ceiling of the car while making a wish and the wish will come true.*
  (See RAINBOW, TALK)

Broom

- *If you buy a broom in* MAY,
  You will sweep your luck away.
- *Always sweep something into a house with a new broom before you use it to sweep anything out of the house.*
- *If you use a broom to sweep dust out of the front door of your house, you will sweep all your friends away.*
- *A girl who steps over a broom handle will be a bad house-keeper.*
- *A girl who steps over a broom will not marry or will have an unhappy marriage.*
- *Put a fork in an upside-down broom to drive unwanted guests away.*

(See MOP, SWEEPING)

Butter • To make butter come quickly when you are churning, say this CHARM:

> *Come, butter, come.*
> *Johnny stands at the gate*
> *Waiting for a buttered cake.*
> *Come, butter, come.*

Buttercup • *If you hold a buttercup under a friend's chin, and the yellow of the buttercup shines on the skin, everything the friend says will be true.*

In some places the reflection can be used to tell if the person is angry or in love. (See JEALOUSY)

Butterfly • *If you bite the head off of the first butterfly you see in a year, you will have good luck all year.*
- *If the first butterfly you see in the year is white, you will have good luck all year.*
- THREE *butterflies together mean good luck.*

Button • *If you put a button into the wrong hole, some misfortune will happen to you during the day.*
To stop the bad luck caused by the wrong buttoning, take the piece of clothing off and put it on again.
- *Buttons exchanged by friends or received as gifts are good luck.* Good luck AMULETS are sometimes made by stringing a necklace or bracelet of buttons exchanged with friends or gotten as a gift. As long as the buttons are worn, the friendship cannot be broken.
- To find out what your occupation will be, say the following while counting your buttons:

> *Rich man,*
> *Poor man,*
> *Beggarman,*
> *Thief.*
> *Doctor,*
> *Lawyer,*
> *Merchant,*
> *Chief.*

In England the counting goes

> *Tinker, tailor, soldier, sailor,*
> *Gentleman, apothecary,*
> *Plowboy, thief.*
> *Soldier brave, sailor true,*
> *Skilled physician, Oxford blue,*
> *Learned lawyer, squire so hale,*
> *Dashing airman, curate pale.*
> *Army, Navy,*
> *Medicine, Law,*
> *Church, Nobility,*
> *Nothing at all.*

(See LETTER)

- *Never button new* CLOTHES *before they have been worn.*
- *If a woman makes a wish about a man's future the first time she sews a button on for him, the wish will come true.*
- *Do not pick up a black button you find on the road or you will become ill.*

  Black buttons or pebbles are sometimes left by people who think they have become sick because of witchcraft. The sickness passes to the person who picks the button up.

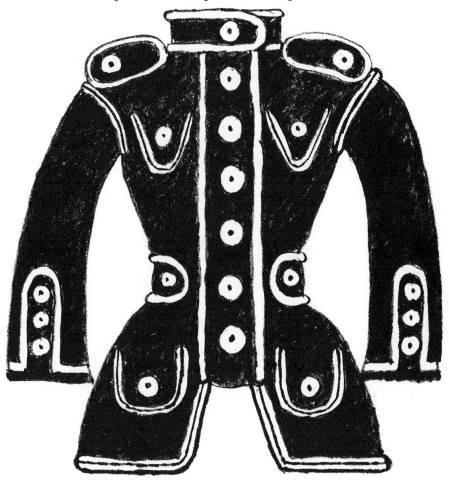

Buying • *When you are buying anything alive, it is good luck for the animal if you return a small part of the purchase price.*

Cake • *Cake batter should always be stirred in a* CIRCLE, *clockwise, or the cake will be spoiled.*

Camphor • *A camphor ball worn in a cloth bag around the neck will protect a child from serious illness.*

Candle • *If a candle lighted as part of a religious ceremony blows out, it is a sign that evil spirits are nearby.*
• *If a candle burns* BLUE *it is a sign that a good spirit is nearby.*
• *A candle should be lighted at every important event.*
Fire was once necessary everywhere to protect people from cold, dark, and wild animals. Candles were often used as a symbol of protection once the need for real fire was gone. Since evil spirits were thought likely to be present at important events, bonfires and, later, candles became part of all celebrations. In some places bonfires are still lit on Halloween, May 1, and the birthdays of important people. (See BIRTHDAY CAKE, DEATH)
• To bring your lover to you, stick two pins through a candle. By the time the candle burns down to the pins, your lover will arrive. While sticking the pins in the candle, say the following CHARM:

> *It is not this candle alone I stick*
> *But my love's heart I mean to prick.*
> *If (Name) be asleep or (Name) be awake*
> *I'll have (Name) come to me and speak.*

Candlemas Day
> *If Candlemas Day is fair and clear,*
> *There will be two winters in the year.*

Candlemas Day, celebrated in England, is February 2.
(See GROUNDHOG DAY)

Car • *Washing a car will bring rain.*

Cat • *If a cat sneezes it is a sign of rain.*
• *Cats born in the month of May cannot catch rats or mice.*
• *Carrying a cat into the house brings bad luck.*
   The cat should be allowed to walk into the house by itself.
• *If a cat sneezes* THREE *times there will soon be a cold in the family.*
• *A cat will try to take the breath from a newborn child.*
   (See SNEEZE)
• *It is unlucky to let a cat die in the house.*
• *A cat has* NINE *lives.*
   In parts of China, parents used to embroider a cat's head on the shoes of a child just learning to walk. It was thought that this would make the child as surefooted as the cat.
• *A cat will stay at home if you butter its paws.*
• *If a man accidentally steps on a cat's tail, he will marry before the year is out.*
• If a man asks a woman to marry him, and she is not sure, she may "leave it to the cat." Three HAIRS are taken from a white cat's tail and folded in a white paper. The paper is then put under the woman's doorstep. In the morning the paper is unfolded with care being taken out to shake or move the hairs. If the hairs are crossing each other the answer is yes. If the hairs are not touching, the answer is no.
   (See BLACK CAT, FEVER, FIRE, PHOTOGRAPH)

Cemetery • *You must hold your breath while going past a cemetery or you will breathe in the spirit of someone who has recently died.* (See SNEEZE)
   (See CHRISTMAS, ST. MARK'S EVE)

Chair • *It will bring on a fight if you spin a chair on one leg.*
To take away the trouble, spin the chair THREE times in the opposite direction.

• *If a girl knocks a chair over she will stay single for at least a year.*
In some places in the United States, a girl must be very careful not to knock over a chair when she has enemies present. If she does, they may start to count and not stop until she has righted the chair and is sitting in it. The number they reach is the number of years that will go by until she will marry.
(See NURSE)

Charms • A charm is a way of bringing good luck or protecting against bad luck with words and/or gestures. ABRACADABRA is a charm of words. To CROSS your fingers is a charm of gesture. To cure burns, some people say the following charm:

> *Two angels came from the west.*
> *One brought fire,*
> *The other frost.*
> *Out fire, in frost.*

Cheeks • *If your cheeks suddenly feel on fire, someone is talking about you.*
(See DIMPLE)

Children • *To step over a child crawling on the floor is to stop the child's growth.*

• *A child should not be called by its NAME until it is christened.*

• *A child should wear a piece of IRON on a string around its neck for the first two years of life to keep safe from witches and fairies.*
(See BABY, PREGNANCY)

Chopsticks • *A gift of chopsticks to a newly married couple is a wish that children will soon be born.*
• *To drop a chopstick means that you will soon have a visitor.*
• *If you drop two chopsticks you will soon take a trip.*
• *If you find an unmatched pair of chopsticks at your place you will miss your next train, ship, bus, or plane.*
(See FORK, KNIFE)

Christmas • *To ensure good luck for the coming year, the first person to enter the house on Christmas morning should be a male.*
This superstition, or one like it, is found in many Christian countries. To be sure that a man is the first to enter the house, groups of men, carrying an image of Jesus, sometimes go from house to house early in the morning.
• *Christmas decorations must be taken down by January 6 or* BAD LUCK *will follow.*
In the Christian calendar, January 6—Epiphany—is celebrated as the day of the coming of the Magi.
• *It is bad luck to burn the evergreens used for Christmas decorations.*
• HOLLY *used for Christmas decorations should be saved to keep the house safe from lighting.*
• *A* GREEN *Christmas makes for a crowded cemetery.*
(See LETTER)

Christmas Eve • GHOSTS *never appear on Christmas Eve.*
• *Bees hum the One Hundredth Psalm on Christmas Eve.*
(See ANIMALS, HOLLY)

Cigarettes • *It is bad luck to light* THREE *cigarettes on a single match.*
It is often said that this superstition started in the trenches during the First World War. Snipers would see the first cigarette being lit, take aim on the second, and fire on the third. The superstition, however, was known during the Crimean War many years before World War I.

It may go further back than that and have nothing at all to do with snipers. Priests in the early Eastern Orthodox Church forbade anyone but churchmen to light three candles from a single flame in church. Anyone who did so was punished, and so three lights from one flame became bad luck.

Circles • *Evil spirits cannot harm you when you are standing inside a circle.*
• *Evil spirits cannot pass through a circle.*
• *All circles should be drawn as the* SUN *moves.*
• *You can break bad luck by turning* SEVEN *times in a sunwise circle.*

Superstitions about circles come from the days when the sun was worshipped. The sun was thought to move around the earth in a huge circle, and so circles became important as symbols of the sun. Lipstick was first worn by Egyptian women not to make themselves look beautiful, but to keep evil spirits from entering the mouth and to stop the soul from leaving through the mouth. The lipstick circle, using the power of the sun, formed a protective barrier. (See EYE SHADOW)

People thought that it was a sign of respect to the sun to do things in the direction that the sun moves, from east to west, or what we now think of as clockwise. Circle dances always started sunwise, circles were drawn as the sun moves, and, certainly, all good CHARMS had people moving with the sun. (See CAKE)

Hold your breath while going past a cemetery or you will breathe in the spirit of someone who has recently died.

Clock • *If a clock which has not been working suddenly chimes, there will be a death in the family.*
• *It is bad luck to have more than one working clock in a room.*
• *A clock stops when its owner dies.*

Clothes • *When you put on a new coat, put* MONEY *in the righthand pocket at once to ensure your pocket always being full.*
• *If you have your clothes mended while you are wearing them you will soon die.*
Only the clothing of the dead is sewn on a body. If clothing must be sewn on a living person, that person should chew a piece of thread from the spool in use while the sewing is being done. The chewing shows the devil that the person is still alive and cannot be taken away yet.
• *If you sew clothes on a person, you will sew up the wearer's brains.*
As in the superstition above, the harm can be stopped by chewing a piece of the thread being used. In this case the chewing keeps the brain moving.
• *If you have your clothes mended while you are wearing them, rumors will be spread about you.*
• *If you accidentally put on a piece of clothing inside out as you get dressed in the morning, you will have success in all you do throughout the day.*
• *Clothes worn inside out will protect against witches.*
(See BACK, BUTTON, DOORKNOB, DRESS, SHOES, SOCKS)

Cobweb • *It is unlucky to destroy a cobweb.*
It was believed that a spider spun a web to hide the infant Jesus in the manger when the messengers of Herod came to look for him.
(See ASTHMA, INITIALS)

Coffeepot • *It is bad luck to set up housekeeping with a new coffeepot.*

Coin • *When you find a coin,* SPIT *once on each side of it to drive away the bad luck of the person who lost it.*
Tossing a coin in the air to decide an issue started when people believed that the gods decided if a coin fell with head or tail up. Some people now believe that a force called luck guides the coin.
(See MONEY, PENNY)

Comb
• *If you comb your* HAIR *after dark, You'll comb sorrow into your love's heart.*
• *Never comb your hair when it is wet or you'll comb the devil into it.*
• *To drop a comb while you are combing your hair is a sign of a coming disappointment.*
The disappointment can be stopped by counting backwards from SEVEN while picking up the comb.

Conch shell • *A conch shell will bring bad luck if it is used as a decoration inside a house.*

Copper • *Bracelets made of copper can protect the wearer against arthritis and rheumatism.*

Coral • *Illnesses of the blood can be cured by wearing coral.*
• *Teething rings made of coral can protect babies from illness.*

Cornbread • *Cornbread should always be broken, never cut with a knife.*
If cornbread is cut with a KNIFE, the next year's corn crop will be cut in half.

Cornerstone • When building a building, it is considered lucky to put special objects inside the walls. The most common place for the objects is in the cornerstone— the bottom stone where two walls meet. Originally the builders buried treasure, food, or even living people to gain the goodwill of the gods of the ground. Now we bury historical records or items connected with the use of the building.

Corpse • *Each corpse buried in a graveyard must leave its soul in this world to keep guard until another corpse is buried.*
(See BODY, DEATH, DROWNING, MURDERER, SHIP)

Cough • To cure a cough, take a HAIR from your head, roll it into a ball with some honey, and feed it to a dog saying the following CHARM:

> *Eat well you hound,*
> *May you be sick*
> *and I be sound.*

(See AMBER, CAT, MOUSE, OAK TREE, ONIONS)

Counting • *If you count people, you will endanger the life of one of them.*
People should be counted only by the devil, so that he may take his due, or by God on the Day of Judgment. Instead of counting people, count the number of shoes and divide by two, or count an article of clothing which each person is wearing.
(See BUTTON, NUMBERS, STARS)

Crack • *Step on a crack, break your mother's back.*
The crack was thought to represent the opening of a grave. To step on the grave was to call death to your family. In some places the superstition says "break your grandmother's back." (See WEDDING COUPLE)
• *If you do not step on the last crack before you go into the school building you will fail in your lessons that day.*

Cradle • *If you rock an empty cradle, the cradle will be filled within a year.*

Cramp • *To cure a cramp, put your right shoe across the cramp.*
• *If you wear a* RING *made from the hinge of a used coffin, you will never have a cramp.*
• *You will get stomach cramps if you eat bread from a loaf while it is still hot from the oven.*

Cricket • *A cricket in the house brings good luck.*
The Japanese, the English, and some tribes of American Indians honored the cricket. They thought that it brought good luck to the house and took luck with it when it left.

Crops • *Crops planted in the full of the* MOON *will grow faster than crops planted when the moon is on the decrease.* Vegetables which grow underground—beets, ONIONS, POTATOES, carrots, radishes—are planted only during the dark of the moon. Crops which grow above ground—PEAS, tomatoes, beans, PUMPKIN, and squash—are planted only in the light of the moon. Crops are gathered in the same phases of the moon in which they were planted. The new moon and the day before it are sometimes called "blind days." Some people thought that nothing should be planted on these days and that no important task should be started then.
(See ANIMALS, FEBRUARY 14)

Cross • The cross, as a sign against evil, goes much further back than the Christian era. As an object or a gesture made by hand, the cross has long been thought to cure illness, protect against misfortune, and drive off evil spirits. Crosses may have originally been symbolic of the four directions or of the four elements—fire, water, earth, and sky. Making the sign of the cross in the air is part of many CHARMS, and some charms can only work when performed at a crossroad. (See FOUR-LEAF CLOVER, SHAKING HANDS)

- *Cross your fingers to avoid bad luck, to make wishes come true, or to stop what you say from coming true.*

  Crossing fingers is one of the most common ways of making the sign of the cross. The fingers may be crossed by putting the second finger of the right hand on top of the first finger of that hand. Or you can make a cross by putting the second knuckle of the first finger of your right hand on top of the second knuckle of the first finger of your left hand. The fingers should be at right angles. Keep the fingers crossed while making a wish or in the presence of evil. The wish and the evil get trapped where the fingers cross. Be sure to keep your fingers crossed long enough to let the good spirits do their work.

Crows

- *One's bad,*
  Two's luck,
  THREE's *health,*
  Four's wealth,
  Five's sickness,
  Six is death.
  (United States)

In England MAGPIES are counted instead of crows, but the superstition is much the same.

- *One means anger, two means mirth.*
  Three a wedding, four a birth.
  Five is heaven, six is hell,
  But SEVEN *is the devil's own self.*

  To save yourself from the bad luck which comes from seeing just one crow, bow your head until the bird has gone. If you have a hat on, take it off.

- *Crows gather in large groups when a catastrophe is near.*
  (Bangladesh)

Cuts • *To be sure that a cut caused by a metal instrument heals well, clean the instrument carefully and keep it clean.* (Southern United States)

In the islands of the South Pacific, people are very careful not only to clean the instrument but also to guard it from any enemies who might dirty it on purpose to make the cut heal badly. The superstition is based on the belief that the BLOOD on the instrument continues to feel with the blood in the body.

Dandelion • *If you pick dandelions you will wet your bed.*
(See WEATHER)

Darkness • *Dark air brings bad health.*
The dark has often been thought to be the home of evil spirits. Dark air, the air after sundown, was thought to be dangerous because it might hide evil spirits. If the air were breathed in, the spirits might be also, and the result might be sickness. Windows were not opened at night and unless it was necessary, no one walked outside after dark. The fear of dark air still exists in some parts of England, northern Europe, and the United States. (See NIGHT AIR)

Daughter

• *First a daughter, then a son,*
And the world is well begun.

Day • If you believe it to be a day earlier or later in the week than it is, you will gain or lose a friend.

• *Lose a day, lose a friend.*
Gain a day, gain a friend.

Death • *If you think you recognize a person approaching you, and then find you have made a mistake, it is a sign that the person you thought you recognized will soon die.*
• *If a warrior dies while asleep, he has met an enemy in a dream and been killed.*

- *The soul of a dying person cannot escape the body to go to heaven if any locks are locked or bolts are bolted in the house.*
- *If there are any KNOTS in the CLOTHES of a corpse when it is put into the coffin, the spirit will not be able to depart for heaven.*

  Locked locks and knots are often used as AMULETS to protect people from death. The Masai, in east Africa, took a HAIR from each child, tied a knot in it, and wore it around their necks as they went into battle or away on a trip. The knots protected the child, not the warriors. The soul of the child was thought to be tied in the knot and unable to escape. Other people believed that evil spirits could not get through knots to harm people. (See FRINGE)
- *If a CANDLE on an altar of a church is blown out by the wind, the minister will soon die.*
- *There are more deaths at low tide than at high tide.*
  This belief is held by almost all peoples living near a coast. (See BEES, CLOCK, MIRROR, NAME, OWL, PARSLEY)

Diamond • A diamond was often worn by a pretty and wealthy woman near her face—around the neck, in the HAIR, in an ear lobe or nostril. The beauty of the diamond was supposed to distract the EVIL EYE from the beauty of the woman and so protect her.
- *A very large diamond brings misfortune to its owner.* (See BIRTHSTONE)

Dimple
- *Dimple on the chin,*
  The devil within.
  Dimple on the cheek,
  A soul mind and meek.
- *A man with a dimple on his cheek will never be a murderer.*

Dishrag • *To drop a dishrag means bad luck is coming.*
The bad luck can be stopped by turning THREE times
with the SUN while throwing a pinch of SALT over your
LEFT shoulder.

Divining rod • *A forked willow branch, held with a fork in
each hand, will dip when it passes over water.*
A divining rod, usually made of willow or another tree
which grows near water, is used throughout the world
to find underground water. In many parts of rural
United States, the well digger doesn't start to work until
the divining rod has chosen the location.

Dog • *It is good luck to have a strange dog follow you.*
• *Dogs know whether or not a person can be trusted.*
• *If a dog passes between a man and a woman who are going to be married, the marriage will have ill luck.*
• *Dogs howling in the dark of night,*
  Howl for death before daylight.
• *If you and your dog share the same pillow, you will also share the same dream.*
  (See WEATHER)

Door • *The back door of a house must be closed before the front door is opened, and the reverse.*
• *Doors should be opened at childbirth to help the mother have an easy delivery.*
  Throughout the world, doors, windows, cupboards, and even boxes have been opened to help in childbirth.
• *It is bad luck to cut a doorway between two rooms after a house is built.*
  (See QUARREL)

Doorknob • *It is bad luck to hang* CLOTHES *from a doorknob.*
  In some places a piece of clothing hanging from a doorknob was a sign to the community that a death had taken place inside the house. To hang clothing from a doorknob when there had been no death would tempt fate.

Dream
• *First night's dream,*
  Second morn told,
  Will come true,
  Ere the month is old.

- *The first dream in a new house or under a new quilt or blanket will come true.*
- *Dream of fruit out of season,*
  Wake to tears without reason.
- FRIDAY *night's dream mark well,*
  Saturday's dream never tell.
- *Dreams at night are the devil's delight*
  Dreams in the morning, heed the angels' warning.
- *To dream of a wedding means death.*
- *To dream of a dance means good fortune.*
- *To dream of* BEES *means bad fortune.*
  Every dream may mean something, but the meanings change from place to place and generation to generation. The only thing that remains the same throughout the world and history is that dreams have always been thought to have meaning.
- To make sure that you have good dreams, always put your LEFT foot on the bed before your right foot when you go to bed at night. At the same time, say the following CHARM:

  > *Left and right,*
  > *Left and right,*
  > *Good dreams all night.*

  (See BIRDS, DOG, LIZARD, NIGHTMARE, QUILT, WEDDING CAKE)

Dress • *The first time you wear a new dress you should be pinched by a friend to bring you good luck.*
- *If the hem of a girl's dress is accidentally turned up, it means that her lover is thinking of her.*
  The girl should kiss the hem and make a wish before turning it down. The wish will come true within a week.
- *You will have bad luck if you put your* LEFT *arm in your dress before your right arm.*
- *If a girl's slip is longer than her dress, it is a sign that her father loves her more than her mother does.*

Drowning • *A person cannot drown before going underwater* THREE *times.*

• *If a gun is fired over the place where a dead* BODY *lies on the bottom of water, the body will float to the top.*

• *A drowned woman floats face up, a drowned man face down.* (See BREAD, CORPSE, EARRING, EGGSHELL, GLASS, SAILOR, SEAL, TATTOO)

Eagle • *To kill an eagle is to act against God and will bring* BAD LUCK.
Adam and Eve did not really die, but were turned into eagles and given an island off the coast of Ireland on which to live.

Earring • *Wearing a gold earring will cure bad eyesight.*
• *A sailor wearing an earring cannot drown.*

Ears • *If your right ear itches or burns, somebody is speaking well of you. If your* LEFT *ear burns, someone is speaking ill of you.*
In Holland it is thought that if you bite your left little finger when your left ear burns the person speaking ill of you will bite his or her tongue.

Easter • *The* SUN *dances as it rises on Easter Sunday.*
• *For good luck throughout the year, wear new clothes on Easter.*
• RED *eggs, planted in the fields on Easter morning, will protect against storms.*

Eating • *If you want clear weather for an important event, you must eat everything on the table at dinner the night before the event.*
(See JOURNEY, THIRTEEN)

Eels • *A* HAIR *from a horse's tail will turn into an eel if it is kept in water.*
• *It takes an eel twelve hours to die, even when cut into small pieces.*

Eggs • *If you wash your hands in the water in which eggs have been boiled, you will get warts.*
(See EASTER, FRIDAY, GOOD FRIDAY, MAY 1)

Eggshells • *You must never leave half an eggshell unbroken or you will have bad luck.*

• *Eggshells must be completely broken after eggs have been eaten or witches will use them for boats, go to sea, and sink ships.*

• *Every eggshell broken saves a sailor from drowning.*

Elbow • *If you kiss your elbow you will turn into a member of the opposite sex.*

Emerald • *An emerald worn near the head can protect against the* EVIL EYE *and eye diseases.*
(See BIRTHSTONE)

Enemy • *To kill an enemy, make a clay figure of him or her. Stick the figure full of* PINS *or nails and put it in a stream with the head toward the current.*

As the water wears the figure away, the enemy will waste away. The same type of CHARM can be worked with wax and fire. The idea of an image of a person acting for the person is widespread. Even today, figures of a hated person are hung to show anger at that person.
(See LIZARD)

Evil Eye • In most of the world it is believed that certain people possess the Evil Eye, a glance which makes them able to kill or cause illness in other persons or animals. Many of the witches who were burned to death in Europe and England in the Middle Ages, and in the United States as late as the 1690s, were accused of having the Evil Eye.

Each country and area has different physical characteristics by which a person with the Evil Eye can be recognized: crossed eyes in one place, a cowlick in another, and even the ability to tame animals in some places.

50

Where most people have blue eyes, brown-eyed people have been accused of having the Evil Eye; in places where most people have brown eyes, the blue-eyed people have been said to have the Evil Eye.

• *To protect yourself from the Evil Eye, you must be very careful never to praise yourself or your family or to call attention to any good fortune.*
Most cultures believe that you call the attention of the Evil Eye if you speak well of yourself or your family. After saying a phrase of praise, Jews will often try to ward off trouble by adding "kineahora," or "I call no evil eye." The Chinese tend to call a bright child stupid or a good-looking one ugly in order to confuse the Evil Eye.

• *To counteract the power of the Evil Eye, collect* NINE *toads, string them alive on one string, and bury them in sacred ground.*
As the toads die, so will the power of the Evil Eye.

• The Greeks believe that an unbaptized child can be protected from the Evil Eye—"mati" in modern Greek— by wearing BLUE beads.

• The Arabic word for the Evil Eye—"el ain"—is not supposed to be said aloud, for fear it will call a person with the Evil Eye to the speaker.
(See DIAMOND, EMERALD, EYE OF GOD, EYE SHADOW, FIG SIGN, POINTING, RABBIT, ROWAN WOOD)

Eyebrows • *People whose eyebrows meet will be lucky in money matters all their lives.*

• *Never trust a man whose eyebrows meet.*

• *If your eyebrows meet above your nose,*
You never will wear wedding clothes.

Eyelashes • Eyelashes are often used for wishing CHARMS. If an eyelash falls out, put it on the back of your LEFT hand and make a wish. Then put the palm of your right hand over the lash and press down. If the lash sticks to your right palm when you raise your hand, the wish will come true. If it stays on your left hand, the wish will not come true. No matter where the eyelash stays, you should always save and hide the eyelash so that no enemy gets hold of it and uses it to work magic against you. (See FINGERNAILS, HAIR, SPIT)

Eye of God • The Eye of God, a diamond-shaped AMULET made of twigs and different-colored yarns, is used by the Huichol Indians in Mexico to protect against the EVIL EYE.

Eyes • *If the eyes of a person who has died are not closed at once, they will look for followers.*
(See HALLOWEEN, ITCH, MURDERER, OPAL, RAIN, WATER)

Eye shadow • Eye shadow was used by ancient Egyptian women to protect them from the EVIL EYE. Black eyeshadow was drawn around each eye to form a CIRCLE that the Evil Eye could not pass through.

Fasting • *Twelve small sips of water, taken just before a fast begins, will help keep thirst away.*

Feathers • *To cure a fever, burn the feathers of a black hen under the patient's bed.*
(See PEACOCK FEATHERS)

February 14 • The fourteenth of February is VALENTINE'S DAY, but it is far more to some people. In England and parts of the United States it is thought that on this day birds and rabbits begin to mate for the year. Others believe that it is unlucky to eat rabbit meat after the fourteenth and until the first harvest MOON in September. To many people in the southern United States, the fourteenth of February is GROUNDHOG DAY, and the weather of the day determines how soon winter will pass. The first planting of lettuce should be done before daylight on the fourteenth or no lettuce will grow that year. Peas should also be planted on February 14, but not until the moon rises.

Feet • *To meet a man with flat feet on Monday morning is bad luck.*
In order to stop the bad luck, you must return home, eat and drink something, and start the day again.
• *If the bottom of your right foot itches, you are going to take a trip.*
• *It is unlucky to enter a house with the LEFT foot first.*
The left side of the body is thought to hold more evil than the right. The Romans were so concerned that someone might enter their homes on the unlucky left foot that they assigned a man at the door to watch the feet of people entering. The man at the door was called a footman. (See BRIDE)

- *A child born feet first will have the power to heal.*
  In India it was believed that a firstborn child, born feet first, could cure backache by kicking the patient in the back at a crossroad.
- *Lift your feet while driving over a railroad track or a state line and you will have good luck in all your travels.*

Fern • *You will be invisible if you carry a fern seed.*
The belief in fern seeds' ability to make people invisible is widespread and probably due to a lack of understanding of plant life. At first it was thought that the fern had no seed. Later people realized that it was silly to think that there could be a plant without a seed; they believed that the fern had an invisible seed. Still later a more knowledgeable generation thought that the seed was not invisible, but that it only existed at midnight on Midsummer Eve. (Midsummer Eve is the day before the first day of summer.) A person who could catch the seed in a white cloth before it touched the ground would gain the power to become invisible.
(See RAIN)

Fever • *To cure a fever, take a piece of clean cloth, tie* THREE KNOTS *in it, and rub the patient's forehead with the cloth. Then place the cloth in running water.*
The fever will be caught by the knots and then passed into and carried away by the water.
- *If someone in the family is ill with a fever, wash the patient, throw the water over a cat, and chase the cat outside.*
The cat will take the fever with it.
(See ABRACADABRA, FEATHERS, ONION, PEPPER, RABBIT, SOLOMON'S SEAL, SUNDAY)

Fig sign • The fig sign is used to avoid evil or bad luck when you have done something which could attract bad spirits or the EVIL EYE. You would make the fig sign, for example, if you walked under a LADDER or if you praised a member of your family. The fig sign is made by making a fist and putting your thumb up between your index finger and your middle finger.

Finger • *If you can touch the forefinger and the little finger of your* LEFT *hand over the back of your hand, you will be a good cook.*

• *If the forefinger of the right hand is used to put on medicine, the wound will never heal.*

• Witches were thought to point with the right forefinger while cursing their victims. (See POINTING)

• *To help in healing, all medicines should be put on with the* RING *finger of the* LEFT *hand.*

(See CROSS, FIG SIGN, V SIGN, WEDDING BAND)

Fingernails • *It is bad luck to cut your fingernails on Friday or Sunday.*

• *Monday is the best day to cut fingernails, and people who always do so will always have money.*

• A girl can get her boyfriend to visit her on Sunday by cutting her fingernails on Saturday while saying the following CHARM:

> *Dullix, ix, ux.*
> *I hold my love's luck.*
> *As these nails go,*
> *Let his face show.*
> *Dullix, ix, ux.*

• *Never cut your fingernails in order.*
To do so is to invite death, since nails on a corpse are always cut in order.

• *Fingernail parings should be saved, burned, or buried, but never scattered outside.*
Fingernail parings were used in many CHARMS and curses to cause or cure illness. In many places—from Thailand to Germany—fingernail parings have been

kept in special ways to save them from use in evil doings.
(See EYELASHES, HAIR, SPIT)
* *White specks on fingernails mean good fortune.*
* *White specks on fingernails show how many lies you have told.*
* *Specks on the fingers,*
  Money lingers;
  Specks on the thumbs,
  Money comes.

Fire • *A small child who plays at the fire will wet the bed that night.*
* *A fire that is in a direct line with the rays of the* SUN *will not burn well.*
* *Never look directly into a fire when it is being kindled or it will not burn right and will bring ill luck to the whole family.*
* *A three-colored* CAT *will keep a house safe from fire.*
* *It is bad luck to poke at or add fuel to another person's fire.*
  (See CANDLE, CROSS, POKER, SEAWEED)

Fish • *If you eat many fish you will increase the size of your brain.*
This is a fairly modern superstition. About one hundred years ago it was found that fish have a lot of a chemical called phosphorus in them, and that the brain does also. It was therefore thought that fish would be good food for the brain.
* *A fish should always be eaten from the head towards the tail.*
Eating a fish from head to tail forces fish still in the water to swim toward the shore and the fishermen.

Fishing · *It is bad luck to say the word "pig" while fishing at sea.*
The Scottish fishermen who believe this superstition
also believe that the bad luck can be stopped by touching
a piece of IRON and saying "Cold iron."
· *If you count the number of fish you have caught, you will
catch no more that day.*
· *If the fish are not biting, one of the fishermen should be
thrown into the water and hauled out again. The fish will
then begin to bite.*
(See MOON)

Fits · *To cure fits, go to a church at midnight, walk THREE
times up each aisle and then once around the church in the
direction of the SUN.*
· *To cure fits, collect a PENNY from each of twelve maidens,
melt the pennies and have them made into a RING. The ring
should be worn forever on the middle finger of the LEFT hand.*

Flag · *It brings bad luck for a flag to touch the ground.*
Throughout most of history, flags were carried into battle
and kept near the king as a sign that he was unharmed.
When the flag was captured or knocked to the ground,
the enemy was dangerously near the king.

Fleas · *Fleas never go near a person who is about to die.*

Flowers · *Flowers should not be brought into a house out of
their season or bad luck will come into the house before the
flowers die.*
· *Red and white flowers in a vase in the room of a sick person
will bring death.*
The flowers should either be put into two separate
vases, or flowers of a third color should be added.
· *Flowers, given as a gift, bring good luck to giver and receiver.*

Fog • *When fog rises rapidly, it is a sign of rain to come.*
(United States)
• *Fog goes up with a hop,*
Rain comes down with a drop.
(Scotland)
• *If fog seems to go down into the ground, there will be several*
days of clear weather.
(See SNOW)

Food • *If you are given a gift of food, the container in which*
it was given should not be returned empty.
To return the container empty might bring hunger to the
house of the giver or the receiver.
• *Hot food is more nourishing than cold food.*
(See FORK, PREGNANCY, QUARREL)

Footprint • *The devil can trap people with dust taken from*
their LEFT footprints.
Women in the Sahara Desert wear long, sweeping cloaks
to wipe out their footprints and thus escape the devil.

Fork • *To drop a fork means that a man is coming to visit.*
If food drops at the same time the fork does, it means
that the visitor will be hungry when he arrives.
(See BROOM, CHOPSTICKS, KNIFE)

Four-leaf clover • *A four-leaf clover will bring good luck to*
one who finds and carries it.
A four-leaf clover probably became a good luck symbol
because it is rare and looks like a CROSS, not the cross of
Jesus—the superstition goes back before the Christian
era—but the sun cross. The sun cross represented the
four directions: east to west and north to south. The
Druids of ancient England, who worshipped the SUN,
thought that the four-leaf clover gave anyone who
carried it the power to see witches and devils. If devils
could be seen, they could be avoided, and that would be
very good luck.

- *Adam and Eve took a four-leaf clover with them when they left the garden of Eden.*
- It is said that this clover has four leaves,

> *One for wealth,*
> *One for fame,*
> *One for health,*
> *One for a faithful lover.*

- *A four-leaf clover given away will not bring luck.*
- *If a young woman finds a four-leaf clover and eats it, she will soon meet her husband-to-be.*

Fox • *To see one fox means good luck, to see several means bad luck.*

In some parts of Europe it was believed that witches going to and from meetings sometimes took the shape of foxes and that these fox-witches always traveled in groups. If you saw more than one fox you might have seen a group of witches.

Freckles • *You can make freckles disappear by washing your face with dew, before dawn, on the first of May. You must wash it* SEVEN *times while facing the place where the* SUN *will rise.*

If the sun does not shine on May 1 you will have freckles for another year.

Friday • *Friday is an unlucky day.*

Friday has been thought unlucky because it was considered to be the day on which Eve tempted Adam, on which the flood started, on which the Temple of Solomon fell, and on which Jesus was crucified. But even in places where the Bible is not read, Friday is thought to be unlucky. In these lands Friday was originally set aside for worship and rest. To work on Friday was to bring bad luck. After Friday stopped being a day of worship for most people, the bad luck of doing certain things on that day stayed with the day. (See FRIDAY THE THIRTEENTH)

• *Any ship that sails on Friday will have ill luck.*
• *You should never start a trip on a Friday or you will meet misfortune.*

The English government once tried to prove how wrong the superstition about Friday was. They started to build a new ship on a Friday, named it the H.M.S. *Friday*, and launched it on a Friday. The new ship started its first voyage on a Friday and was never heard of again.

• *A bed changed on a Friday will bring bad dreams.*
• *Rain on Friday, clear on Sunday.*

- *Hens born of eggs laid on Friday will be tough eating.*
- *Never start to make a garment on Friday unless you can finish it the same day or it will bring ill luck when worn.*

Friday the thirteenth • *A* FRIDAY *which is also the thirteenth day of the month is always unlucky.*

The special bad luck that is supposed on fall on Friday the thirteenth is probably just a combination of the superstitions about Friday and about the number THIRTEEN. Some people say, however, that Friday the thirteenth became unlucky because there are twelve WITCHES and one devil at each meeting of witches, and all meetings are on Friday.

- *If you were born on the thirteenth of any month, Friday the thirteenth is an especially lucky day for you.*

Fringe • Fringe was once placed on garments, especially those used in worship, to keep evil spirits away. It was thought that the spirits would get tangled in the fringe and not be able to get to the person. Sometimes KNOTS were put in the fringe to further confuse and trap the spirits. Because knots can be a source of trouble, the knots in the fringe of the prayer shawl worn by orthodox Jews spell out one of the sacred NAMES of God. In this manner, possible bad luck is overcome.

Frog • *A frog brings good luck to the house it enters.*
(See ASTHMA)

Frying pan • *An empty frying pan left on the fire causes wrinkles on the face of the owner.*
(See PREGNANCY)

Funeral • *If you meet a funeral procession, you must accompany it for a little way or you will tempt the devil to take you.*
• *The soul from the first funeral performed in a new church is claimed by the devil.*
• POINTING *at a funeral procession will cause you to die within the month.*
(See RAIN)

Furniture • *It is unlucky to be the one who removes the tag from furniture.*
All pieces of upholstered and stuffed furniture have a fabric tag which lists the materials used in construction. On the tag is a notice that the tag is not to be removed under penalty of law. Although the instruction is meant for the seller, not the buyer, of the furniture, it is often considered illegal, and unlucky, to be the one who removes the tag.

Gambling • *Borrowed* MONEY *cannot lose.*
Because of this belief, no gambler will ever lend another gambler money when they are playing in the same game or betting on the same thing.

• *To change your luck at the gambling tables, walk* THREE *times around your chair in the direction of the* SUN. (See LUCK)

Garlic • *Hang garlic around the house on Halloween to keep evil spirits away.*

• *Wear a necklace of garlic buds while sleeping to keep evil away and to stop your soul from leaving your body.*
Evil spirits were thought to dislike the smell and taste of garlic. In almost every place that garlic is raised, there are superstitions about its ability to protect from evil and illness. (See JAUNDICE, ONIONS)

Gate • *It is unlucky to close a gate left open by someone else.* (See HEADACHE, KISS)

George • *No man named George has ever been hanged.*

Ghosts • *To protect yourself from ghosts, make a* CROSS *from two pieces of fruit wood tied together with* RED *thread. Wear the cross between the lining and the material of your coat.*

• *If you meet a ghost,* SPIT *on the ground between you and say, "In the name of the Lord, what do you wish?" The ghost will disappear.*
This CHARM works only with the ghosts of human beings.

Ginger • *If you eat ginger or other hot spices before saying a* CHARM, *your charm will be "heated" and have special power.*

Glass • *When a glass is accidentally hit, the high note that sounds is the voice of a drowning sailor.*

• *When making a toast, glasses must be clinked together to stop the evil spirits from opposing the toast.* (See NOISE)
An old English and American Jewish superstition says that if a glass or dish is broken, everyone present must call out "mazel tov" or clap to change the bad luck into good. (See STARS)

Gold • Gold has often been used to make AMULETS in parts of South America. Some early Indian tribes worshipped the SUN and believed that gold was the tears of the sun-god.

Golf • *When teeing off, the ball should be placed so that the trade name or number is facing up or the hole will be lost.*

• *To say the word "socket" on a golf course brings bad luck.* One of the worst faults in golf is to hit the ball with the socket of the club. Golfers, like most athletes, are extremely superstitious—since luck appears to play such a large part in winning or losing. Many have individual rites, such as not washing just before a match or a game, or always wearing a lucky shirt. Other athletes carry AMULETS which they touch at important points of play, and some refuse to wear a certain color. (See BASEBALL, BASKETBALL, RACES, TENNIS)

Good Friday • *A loaf of bread baked on Good Friday will never become moldy.*

• *A hot CROSS bun baked on Good Friday will stay fresh if saved for a year. As long as the bun stays fresh, it will protect sailors from the house from drowning.*
Crosses, made with icing or cut with a knife, were often put on foods to keep them safe from evil. Such food was especially popular on holidays when many evil spirits were thought to be around.

• *A RING blessed on Good Friday will prevent illness as long as it is never removed.*

- *Planting done on Good Friday will come up well.*
- *Eggs laid on Good Friday will go bad quickly.*

Graves • *Graves on the south side of the church or cemetery are the holiest.*
- *Pointing at a grave will make your finger rot.*
- *If you suddenly shiver, someone is walking over the spot where your grave will be.*

Green • *It is bad luck to wear green on a stage.*
- *To wear green to a christening brings bad luck to the child who is being baptized.*
- *Green's forsaken,*
  YELLOW *is forsworn.*
  BLUE's *the color*
  That should be worn.

Green is thought to be the color of the clothes of the "little people." Wearing green on special occasions invites the elves to the gathering and gives them power over the people there. (See LOVERS, WEDDING DRESS)

Groundhog Day • The groundhog wakes up from its winter's sleep on February 2 and comes out of its underground nest. If it is a sunny day and the groundhog is frightened by its own shadow, it will go back underground and there will be six more weeks of winter. If it is a cloudy day, and there is no shadow, the groundhog comes out to play and spring will soon arrive. (See CANDLEMAS DAY, FEBRUARY 14)

Guest • *To make an unwelcome guest leave your house, put a pinch of pepper under the guest's chair.*
- *If you watch until a departing guest is out of sight, you will never meet again.*
(See BED, BROOM, HANDS, ITCH, NAPKIN, TALK, VISITOR)

Hair • *Hair clippings or combings can be used by witches and other evil ones to cast spells.*

The importance of hair clippings and combings shows in the superstitions of peoples in many lands. In Egypt it was believed that hair and nail clippings plus a drop of a person's BLOOD could give an enemy complete control over that individual. (See EYELASHES, FINGERNAILS, SPIT) Indians in ancient Peru, as well as more modern peoples, believed that all hairs should be kept, since people would be responsible for them on Judgment Day. To give someone you love a lock of your hair is a sign of great trust, since the hair could be used to do you great harm.

• *If cut or combed-out hair is allowed to blow away and is used by a bird to built a nest, the head from which the hair came will ache or develop sores or dandruff.*
• *If a* CROW *uses your hair to build its nest, you will die within a year and a day.*
• *Hair cut while the* MOON *is on the increase will grow faster.*
• *Hair which burns brightly when thrown into the fire means long life for the person from whose head the hair came.*
• *If you pull out a gray hair, ten more will grow in its place.*
• *Trust no man,*
  Even your own brother,
  Whose hair is one color
  And beard is another.
• *A hairy chest is a sign of strength.*
• *Curly hair is lucky hair.*

In areas of the world where the SUN was worshipped, curly hair was thought to look like the rays of the sun. The curls formed a wavy CIRCLE around the human head the way the sun was believed to move around the earth.

Curly hair was thus thought to be a sign of the sun-god's favor.

- *Eating bread crusts will make hair curly.*
- *A baby's first bit of cut hair should be rolled into a ringlet and saved for good luck.*
- *If you wrap a lock of your hair and some fingernail clippings in a GREEN leaf, and put them in the ashes of a fire, the ghostly figure of the person you are going to marry will appear in the fireplace.*
  The door must be open and no one must speak while the leaf is burning.
- *A baby whose hair grows quickly will always be weak, since all the baby's strength will go to the hair.*
- *To help cure an illness, cut off the patient's hair so that all the strength will not go into the hair and leave the patient too weak to fight the illness.*
- *We become weak when our hair is cut.*
  (See COMB, RED HAIR, WIDOW'S PEAK)

Halloween • *On Halloween, all the souls in hell are released for forty-eight hours.*
- *If you stand at a crossroad at midnight on Halloween and listen to the wind, you will hear all the important things that are going to happen to you during the coming year.*
- *If you hear footsteps following you on Halloween, you must not turn around, since they are the steps of the dead and if you meet their eyes you will die.*
  (See CANDLE, GARLIC)

Handkerchief • *A gift of a handkerchief between lovers means a parting.*
- *If you find a handkerchief in your path and pick it up, you will soon need it to wipe away your tears.*
- *Birds crying in the night can be silenced by tying KNOTS in opposite corners of an all-white handkerchief.*
  (See MARRIAGE)

Hands • *Warm hands, cold heart.*
• *Cold hands mean a loving spirit.*
• *If two people wash their hands in the same water, they will fight before nightfall.*
In order to break the bad luck, one person must SPIT in the water while the other forms a CROSS by putting the wrist of one arm over the wrist of the other.
• *If the palm of your right hand itches it means you will soon be getting money; if the palm of your LEFT hand itches it means you will soon be paying out money.*
• *If a woman's hand itches at the joint of her right thumb, it means that she will shake hands with an unwelcome guest within an hour.*

Hat • *To put a brimmed hat on backwards is to invite all the bad luck for SEVEN miles.*
• *To put a hat on a bed is to cause bad luck for the house.*
• *If you wear a hat inside a house you will get a headache.*

Headache • *A headache can be cured by being nailed to a TREE.*

"Nailing" a headache or other illness to a tree has been common in many countries. The NAIL was touched to the head or placed under the pillow for a night to give the illness a chance to pass into it. (See IRON) The nail was then nailed into the tree, where the illness was trapped. The type of tree changed from place to place. In some areas, the same tree was used for all people and illnesses. In other places a different tree was used for each person or illness. In ancient Egypt, and in parts of Africa, the headache was nailed to a special town gate or pillar or to the front of a wise man's house. The tree or gate could not be taken down without causing harm to the people who had nailed their illnesses into it.
(See BRAMBLE ARCH, HAIR, HAT, HORSE CHESTNUT, SNAKE, TRACKS)

Headlight • *When you are in a car, and you see another car with only one headlight, hit the palm of your* LEFT *hand with the little-finger-end of the fist of your right hand. You can then either hit or kiss the person you are with.*
Some people say that you must call out the word "padoodle" before anyone else does and that you get to make a wish instead of kissing or hitting.

Heart • A heart-shaped AMULET is thought to provide the wearer with lasting love and to protect against heart disease.
• *It is impossible to* LIE *while you* CROSS *your heart with the index finger of your right hand.*
To try to lie at such a time will bring bad luck and illness, which will last until the lie is confessed.

Heartburn • *Heartburn can be cured by sucking on a piece of coal.*

Hiccups • *To cure hiccups, say the Lord's Prayer backwards.*
• To cure hiccups, say the following CHARM THREE times without taking a breath:

> *Lick up, hiccup,*
> *Stick up, hiccup,*
> *Trick up, hiccup,*
> *Begone, hiccup.*

• *Hiccups in church are a sign of possession by the devil.*

Holly • *Holly should not be brought into the house before Christmas Eve or the family will argue before* CHRISTMAS *morning.*
• *It causes bad luck to step on a holly berry.*
ROBINS, which feed on holly berries, are often considered special birds. To harm their food would be a sign of disrespect and would bring bad luck.

Holy books • The Christian and Jewish Bibles, the Moslem Koran, the Hindu Vedas, and other holy books are often used as powerful AMULETS against evil and illness. In some places people think that is is impossible to lie while holding one hand on such a holy book, and oaths are often taken while touching them. In almost all cultures, it has been believed that if a phrase from a holy book were written on food, and the food eaten, the person who ate the food would gain the power of the phrase. It is likely that our practice of writing "happy birthday" or "good luck" on cakes came from this belief.

Hornets • *If* SEVEN *hornets sting you at one time, you will die before you can count to ten.*
(See WEATHER)

Horse • *If you find braids in your horse's mane in the morning, where there were none the night before, it means that a witch has been riding the horse by night.*
Braids or tangles in a horse's mane are called "witches' stirrups."

• *A horse with four white stockings is lucky; one with only one white stocking is unlucky. The most luck comes from a horse with two white stockings.*
The stocking arrangement of the horse with two white stockings must be exact: One foreleg and one hind leg must be white. One white stockinged leg must be on the off side (the left side when you face the horse) and the other must be on the near side.

- *Four white legs and a long white nose,*
  Take off her hide and throw her to the crows.
- *If a horse yawns, rain will soon come.*
- Horses were often decorated with ribbons, BELLS, and pieces of brass to protect them from harm. The practice of decorating horses continues in many parts of the world. In the United States, horses have their manes braided with colorful ribbons at horseshows and races, a holdover from times when such decorations were thought to protect the animal and bring it luck and speed. (See WHITE HORSE)

Horse chestnut • *If you carry a horse chestnut (a buckeye) in your pocket, you will be protected against rheumatism and headaches.*

- *To carry a horse chestnut in your pocket will bring good luck.*

Horsehair • *No harm can come to you while you are holding a horse's HAIR.*

Horseshoe • A horseshoe is considered a very powerful AMULET. Most often it is nailed to the front of a barn or a house for protection. The shoe must be nailed with the points up, or all the luck will fall out of it. Some of the luck of the horseshoe comes from its being made of IRON, a metal that protects against witches and other evil spirits. The luck of the horseshoe is increased by being nailed onto the horse's foot with SEVEN NAILS.

- *The horseshoe thrown from the near hind leg of a white mare carries the most luck.*
  The near side of a horse is the right side as you face the horse.

- *It is lucky to find a horseshoe on the road.*
  If you do find a horseshoe on the road, pick it up, SPIT on it, throw it over your LEFT shoulder and make a wish. The wish will come true.
- If you find a horseshoe with the closed end toward you, leave it where it is or hang it on a branch of a TREE, saying the following CHARM:

  > *All bad luck for me*
  > *Must hang in that tree.*

  If anyone touches or picks up the hanging horseshoe, the bad luck will pass to that person.
- *A RING made from a horseshoe nail provides the wearer with the same protection that a horseshoe gives.*

House • *You should not move into a new house until SALT, bread, and water have been put inside it.*
- *It is bad luck to move from one house to another in the dark of the MOON.*
  If possible, all moves should be made while the moon is on the increase, so that the family's luck will grow with the moon.
- *A house built ONLY of new materials will bring sickness to those who live in it. Some old lumber or bricks should be used.*
  Not only brides but also houses need "something old." The superstition in both cases may have to do with the fear of the new and the comfort in the old.
- *It is unlucky to enter a new house for the first time by the back door.*

Initials • *If you find your initials in a spider's web you will have good luck forever.*
(See APPLE, BLOOD, MAY 1, OAK TREE, SNAIL)

Insomnia • *To cure insomnia, just before you to go bed put jimsonweed leaves in each of your shoes. Put the shoes under your bed with the toes* POINTING *toward the closest wall.*

Iron • Iron has long been thought to have special and magical qualities. The strength of iron must have come as a surprise to early man: it could break wooden and stone weapons, and could even withstand the all-powerful fire. In ancient Rome, plants which were used in healing could not be touched with iron for fear that the iron would be stronger than the healing properties of the plant. To touch mistletoe, the sacred plant of the Druids, with iron would bring bad luck. Once touched with iron, the plant was no longer holy and could not be used in ceremonies or healing. In other countries, wooden plows were used long after better iron plows became possible. When iron plows were first used in Poland, the harvests were bad for several years, and the use of iron was blamed. (See FISHING)

• *Witches are afraid of iron.*
It was thought that iron was even stronger than the power of witches. A piece of iron nailed to the outside of a house could protect everyone inside the house and could stop elves from stealing the children of the house. Since witches were also thought to be afraid of horses, HORSESHOES which were made of iron were thought to be especially good protection against witches.

- *To bring old iron into the house is to bring bad luck into the house.*

  Old iron, in the form of a NAIL or a horseshoe, could have been used to charm or curse an underworld creature. If the old iron were brought into the house, the curse would come in too.

Ironing • *When ironing anything flat, be careful not to iron in a diamond-shaped fold. Such a fold will bring bad luck to the user of the item.*

Itch • *An itching foot is a sign of travel to a new land.*

- *An itching nose is a sign that you will soon be kissed by a fool.*

- *If your nose itches, if your nose itches,*
  A stranger is coming with a hole in his britches.

- *If your nose itches*
  Your mouth is in danger.
  You'll kiss a fool,
  And meet a stranger.

- *Rub an itch on wood*
  It will come to good.

- *Itch for love on the right,*
  On the LEFT itch for spite,
  But either side is good at night.

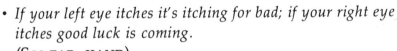

- *If your left eye itches it's itching for bad; if your right eye itches good luck is coming.*
  (See EAR, HAND)

Ivy • *Whooping cough can be cured by drinking tea made from ivy leaves from a cup made of ivy wood.*

Jade • AMULETS made of jade can help protect against stomachaches, bring rain, and make women fertile.

January • *A mild January is bad for man and beast.*

Jaundice • *Jaundice can be cured by rolling a live spider in a little butter and swallowing it.*
In Cuba, jaundice has been said to be cured by wearing THIRTEEN cloves of GARLIC around the neck for thirteen days. In the middle of the night, on the thirteenth day, the wearer must take off the garlic necklace while standing at a crossroad. The necklace should be thrown over the LEFT shoulder and the patient should go home to bed without a backward look.

Jealousy • *To tell if a person is jealous, hold a BUTTERCUP under the chin. If the yellow of the buttercup reflects on the skin, the person is jealous.*

Journey • *To turn back after starting a journey will mean bad luck the rest of the trip.*
If you must turn back for a forgotten object, you can keep the bad luck away by eating and drinking something and then starting off as if for the first time.
(See CHOPSTICKS, FEET, ITCH, TEETH, WHIRLWIND)

June • *June is the luckiest month for weddings.*
June is lucky for weddings only in the Western world. In much of the East, other months are preferred. In Japan, for example, October is the luckiest month for weddings.

Kettle • *A girl who turns the spout of a steaming kettle to the wall will never marry.*

Keys • Keys have often been thought to hold power against evil. They are a way of keeping property safe, and their helpfulness in the human world was thought to extend to the spirit world. In addition, keys were made of IRON and therefore were thought to provide special protection against witches. AMULETS have long been kept with keys so that their combined power could keep both wearer and property safe. In Italy keys are shaken to frighten away evil. (See NOISE) In much of Europe and parts of the United States, an iron key pressed on the back of the neck or under the nose is believed to stop a nosebleed.

Kiss • *Kissing over a gate brings bad luck.*
• *For a man to kiss a girl while she is sitting and he is standing will cause a serious quarrel.*
(See BRIDE, ELBOW, ITCH, MISTLETOE)

Knife • *A knife in your pocket when you are outside at night will keep you safe from witches, elves, and other under world creatures.*
This superstition dates from the days when IRON was thought to protect against evil and the underworld, and most knives were made of iron.

- *If you get a gift of a knife from a lover, it is a sign that the love will soon end.*
- *If you get a present of a knife, you must pay a* PENNY *in return or you will use the knife for evil.*

  Even if the penny is paid, the gift of a sharp object may make the giver and receiver quarrel. To stop the quarrel, both should say the following CHARM:

  > *If you love me, as I love you*
  > *No knife can cut our love in two.*

- *It will start a quarrel if knives are crossed at the table.*

  Crossed knives are a sign of fighting and dueling. To be sure that the quarrel does not start terrible trouble, the person who crossed the knives should uncross them. (See CROSS)

- *Knife falls, gentleman calls;*
  FORK *falls, lady calls;*
  Spoon falls, baby calls.
  (See BIRTH, CHOPSTICK, CORNBREAD)

Knit • *If you knit during important events you will "KNOT" their outcome.*

It is considered especially unlucky to knit on a STAGE or while someone else is taking a test.

Knock on wood • *Knock* THREE *times on wood after mentioning good fortune.*

Knocking on wood, after speaking of good fortune, making a prediction, or boasting, started in the days when TREES were considered to be the homes of good spirits or gods. The gods were asked for favors, and, if the favors were granted, the trees were knocked on as a sign of acknowledgment and thanks. In some places, the knocking was done to make a noise so that the evil spirits who were nearby would not hear of the good fortune and ruin it. (See BREAK, EVIL EYE)

Knots • Women in Scotland have tied knots in their apron strings to protect themselves from accidents. It was thought that the evil spirits would get caught in the knots and not be able to get to the woman. (See DEATH, FRINGE, HANDKERCHIEF)

• To cure warts, make as many knots in a RED string as you have warts. Throw the string away. Whoever picks it up will get the warts and yours will soon disappear. In order to see your love during a dream, say the following CHARM while tying knots in a piece of string.

> *This knot, this knot, this knot I tie,*
> *To see my true love, this knot I tie.*
> *To see my love in his array,*
> *And what he walks in every day;*
> *And if my love be dressed in* GREEN
> *His love for me will not be seen;*
> *And if my love be dressed in* BLUE,
> *His love for me is ever true.*

Then put the string beneath your pillow and sleep on it.

• It is believed that if a verse from a HOLY BOOK is recited while a knot is being tied, the verse will become caught in the knot. The knot can then be used as an amulet.

• Knots can bring misfortune as well as good. (See KNIT) They are thought to be particularly dangerous in the clothing of people who are close to gods and spirits. It is feared that evil spirits will hide in the knots and cause trouble. Priests in many religions have been forbidden to wear knots in their clothing. Clerical collars, rather than neckties, are worn today by Orthodox rabbis and Episcopalian, Greek, and Roman Catholic priests because of this ancient fear of knots.

Ladder • *Walking under a leaning ladder will bring bad luck.*
(See NUMBERS)
A TRIANGLE has long been the symbol of the magic number
THREE. A ladder leaning against a wall forms a triangle,
with the third side being the ground. If you walk
under the ladder you break the triangle and by doing so
challenge the evil one. If you walk under a ladder by
mistake, you can stop the evil one from bringing you
bad luck by forming a CROSS with your fingers and keeping them crossed until you see a dog. Or you can cancel
the bad luck by making the FIG SIGN or by walking backwards to the place where you started. Ladders were
considered lucky by the ancient Egyptians, who used them
as a symbol of rising to the gods. Small ladders were
carried as AMULETS.

Ladybug • *It is bad luck to kill a ladybug.*
If you find a ladybug on you, put it on your palm and
recite the following CHARM. If the ladybug flies away,
you will have good luck.

> *Ladybug, ladybug, fly away home.*
> *Your house is on fire,*
> *Your children all roam.*

Lark • *You can understand a lark's song if you lie on your*
back in a field out of sight of all eyes.

Last breath • *Five minutes pass between the time that a person*
takes a last breath and the time the soul leaves the body.
(See SNEEZE)

Laugh • *It is unlucky to laugh before dawn.*

• *Laugh before light,*
Cry before night.

Leaf • *If you catch a falling leaf on the first day of autumn you will not get a cold all winter.*

Left • The left side of the body is the side of the devil. Many CHARMS work only if done while turning to the right (to avoid the devil) or while motioning to the left (to frighten off the devil). Spilt SALT is thrown over the left shoulder because the devil, or other evil spirits, would stand to the left and the thrown salt might distract them and make them forget to bring bad luck. The Moslems say that each Moslem has two guardian angels on earth. One stands to the right, taking note of good actions, and one to the left, recording bad actions. A Moslem story also says that when God created the world, He threw one handful of dust to the right and the other to the left. From the handful thrown to the right, the people who would be happy were born; from the handful thrown to the left came the people who would be born to an unhappy life.
(See BRIDE, FEET, SHOES)

Letter • *A large hole in your stocking is a sign that you will soon get a letter.*
• *If you find a BUTTON on your path, you will soon get a letter with as many pages as there are holes in the button.*
• *A letter mailed on Christmas Day or February 29 will bring bad luck.*

Lie • There are many CHARMS which are said to prove that a lie is not being told. The best known is

> CROSS *my heart and hope to die,*
> *Cut my throat if I tell a lie.*

• *If someone SNEEZES while another person is making a statement, the statement cannot be a lie.*
(See FINGERNAILS, HEART, HOLY BOOKS, SKULL, TONGUE)

Lightning • *If you use firewood cut from a tree that has been hit by lightning, the house will also be hit by lightning.*
• *Lightning never strikes twice in the same place.*
• *A dog's tail draws lightning to it.*
  (See ACORN, CHRISTMAS, THUNDER)

Lilac • *It is unlucky to pick lilac to take into your house.*

Lizard • *A marriage will not be happy if a lizard crosses the path of the wedding party.*
• *To dream of a lizard is a sign that you have a secret enemy.*

Lovers • To bring your lover to you, put your shoes together on the floor at right angles. The toe of the right shoe should touch the instep of the LEFT. As you are placing the shoes, say the following CHARM:

> *When I my true love want to see*
> *I shape my shoes into a T.*

• The web of a wild duck's right foot, dried and powdered, makes a good love potion. A pinch, placed in a cup of coffee or a glass of milk, will make a person love you forever. If juice is used, however, the love will sour.
• In order to see the face of the person you will love and marry, serve a silent and backward dinner which is measured by the tablespoon instead of the cup. You must walk backward the entire time you are cooking, serving, and eating, and no one can speak the entire time. After you have finished all your food, bow your head over your plate and you will see the face of the one you will love. Some say that the dinner should be served only at midnight. Others say that nothing GREEN should be included in the meal because that color is unlucky for lovers. If you see nothing in your plate it means you will never marry. If you see yourself in a coffin it means you will die before the year is out.
  (See APPLE, BLACK CAT, CANDLE, DRESS, KNIFE, KNOTS, MOON, SNAIL)

Luck • *An actor who is wished good luck in a play will have bad luck.*
• *A rider in a horse show will have bad luck if wished good luck. To bring good luck, say "I hope you break a leg."*
• *To change bad luck into good, pull all your pockets out and turn in a* CIRCLE, *clockwise,* THREE *times.*
• *If you do something that causes bad luck,* SPIT THREE *times to cancel the evil.*
• *A beginner will always have good luck.*
Beginner's luck is based on a belief in the magic of anything new. In this superstition the "new" element is the beginner.
(See BAD LUCK, BREAK, LADDER, RIGHT, ROWAN WOOD)

Magic square • A magic square is an AMULET which allows the wearer or user to control luck or the actions of other people. Most magic squares have rows of numbers arranged so that the sum of each row is equal when added in any direction. (See SQUARE OF SATURN) Some squares use letters rather than numbers and have every row spell the NAME of God or of several gods and spirits. Other magic squares are composed of letters which also stand for numbers. The letters form a wish and the number values of each row is the same, "locking" the wish and ensuring that it will come true. The squares were sometimes embroidered on cloth and worn around the neck to protect the wearer. Sometimes these squares were burned to let the smoke carry the message to the gods. Similar amulets and CHARMS were made in the shape of a TRIANGLE. (See ABRACADABRA)
Magic squares were especially popular in India and the Middle East and in Europe as late as the 1600s. Magic squares and triangles are still used throughout the world, especially to help ward off illness.

16	3	2	13
5	10	11	8
9	6	7	12
4	15	14	1

Magpie • *When you see a magpie,* CROSS *your thumbs and* SPIT *over them or you will have bad luck.*
(See CROWS)

Mandrake • *If you pull a mandrake root out of the ground, you will die at once.*
• *As a mandrake root is pulled from the ground, it shrieks and moans; whoever hears the mandrake will soon go mad.*
The mandrake plant of the Western world is similar to the ginseng of Asia. Both have been important in making love potions and in curing illness. The superstitions about the plants probably arise from the manlike shape of their roots. In the Middle Ages in Europe, dogs were trained to pull the root from the ground so that people could stay where they would not hear the cries of the root.

March
• *If you marry when March winds blow,*
Joy and sorrow you'll both know.

(See NEW YEAR'S EVE, SEEDS)

Marigold • *If you pick marigolds that you have not planted you will take to drink.*

Marriage • *Single girls who walk under a* LADDER *will never marry.*
• *If your first act on* MAY 1 *is to look sideways into a* MIRROR, *you will see the person you are going to marry.*
• *A dropped handkerchief is a sign that its owner is ready to marry.*
(See BACHELOR'S BUTTON, LOVERS, WEDDING BAND, WEDDING CAKE, WEDDING COUPLE)

Matches • *Matches should be removed from a book of matches in such a way as to keep a symmetrical order among even-numbered remaining matches. Failure to do this will cause bad luck before the matchbook is used up.*
(See CIGARETTES, NUMBERS)

May • *It is bad luck to marry in May.*
Because May was the month during which the Romans honored the dead, it was considered an unlucky month for happy events.
(See RAIN, SAGE, SPRING CLEANING)

May 1 • *If you get up before dawn on May 1 and break an egg into a cup of water, you will see the initials of your true love in the water.*
(See FRECKLES, MARRIAGE, NEW YEAR'S EVE, VERTIGO)

Midsummer Day • *If you pick a rose on Midsummer Day and put it away without looking at it again, it will still be fresh on Christmas Day.*
Despite its name, Midsummer Day is celebrated on the first day of summer. (See NEW YEAR'S EVE)

Milk • *It is unlucky to spill milk at the table, but you can change the luck by saying an enemy's NAME THREE times.*
• *If there are bubbles on the top of your glass of milk, and you can drink the milk before the bubbles break, you will get money within the number of days there were bubbles.*
(See TEA, THUNDER, WHOOPING COUGH)

Mirror • *To break a mirror means SEVEN years' bad luck.*
It was long thought that a person's reflection was the person's soul. To break the reflection was to harm the soul. At first the reflections were in water, later in polished metal, and then in a mirror. (See BABY) The bad luck can be stopped by burying the pieces of the mirror or by washing them in a stream flowing south.
• *It is unlucky to see your face in a mirror by candlelight.*
• *If a mirror in a house falls and breaks of its own accord, someone in the house will die shortly.*
• *The mirrors in a house where someone has died should be covered.*
In many parts of the world—India, America, China, Africa, and Europe—mirrors have been, and probably

still are, covered after a death. If they were not covered, the ghost of the newly dead could gather up the souls reflected in the mirrors and take them away to heaven or hell. In some places it was thought that if the soul saw its body it would never know peace.

• *A witch's image is not reflected in a mirror, since a* WITCH *has no soul.*

• *A mirror which is framed only on* THREE *sides has been used by a witch to see over long distances.*

Mistletoe • *It is bad luck to refuse a* KISS *while standing under mistletoe.*

• *To use mistletoe in church decorations will bring bad luck.* Mistletoe was banned in churches because it was sacred to the Druids, the high priests of one of the major religions in England at the time Christianity was first introduced in that country. Many "new" religions claim that the sacred objects of existing religions bring bad luck. (See IRON)

Moles • *A mole on the back of the neck is a sign that the person will be hanged.*

• *A mole on your arm*
Can do you no harm.
A mole on your lip,
You're witty and flip.
A mole on your neck
Brings money by the peck.
A mole on your back
Brings money by the sack.
A mole on your ear
Brings money year by year.

- *It is unlucky to have more moles on the* LEFT *side of your body than on the right side.*
- *An oblong mole brings bad luck.*
- A HAIR that grows from a mole on the right side of the body can be pulled out and used as an AMULET.

Money • *A bridegroom should give a* BRIDE *a* COIN *to put in her shoe before the wedding to bring good fortune to the marriage.*
- *Never refuse to give a beggar money—at least a* PENNY—*or the beggar's misfortune will fall on you or a loved one.*
- *Take the first money you receive each day,* KISS *it, then* SPIT *on it, and then put it in an empty pocket and it will draw more money.*

  The first money of the day, in the English market towns, is often still treated this way. The money is called "handsel." Handsel money should also be placed in the pocket of new coats or CLOTHES, or in new pocketbooks when they are first worn or given as a gift.

- *Money, money, come to me*
  Before the day is less;
  I see polka dots
  On a lady's dress.

- To be sure that you will always have money, carry a bent coin, or one with a hole in it at all times. Take it out only at the new MOON. Then SPIT on it and turn it around THREE times before you put it back in your pocket. If you change clothes, change the coin without looking at it. If you don't carry a special coin, you should use the new-moon CHARM with any new coin in your pocket in order to increase your money.

  (See HANDS, MILK, MOLE, RUST, SHOES, SPIDER, SWEEPING, TWO-DOLLAR BILL)

If you refuse to give money to a beggar, the beggar's misfortune
will fall on you or a loved one.

Moon • The SUN may be all-powerful, but the moon is most mysterious. Ever changing, ever beautiful, the moon is the center of more superstitions than anything else. Even today, many people in every part of the world believe in and follow superstitions about the moon. Since the earliest time, the phases of the moon have been carefully watched and named. The "dark" of the moon is the time from the full moon to the new moon. During this period the moon is said to be on the decrease, or waning.

The other half of the moon's cycle—from the new moon to the full moon—is called the "light" of the moon. During that time the moon is on the increase, or waxing. The crescent moon, when the moon is on the increase, is thought to be good luck for lovers and travelers. An AMULET in the shape of the crescent moon—with the points to the LEFT as they are in an increasing moon—is said to protect against evil on a journey.

Many farmers, even modern ones with the most up-to-date tools, have superstitions about planting and gathering CROPS according to the phases of the moon. Lives, as well as crops are sometimes arranged according to the phases of the moon. Business projects are best started when the moon is on the increase, so that MONEY can increase along with the moon. The digging of the foundation of a HOUSE or a well would best be started in the dark of the moon; otherwise the construction will not sit well in the ground. Boards cut in the light of the moon are supposed to decay faster than those cut in the dark of the moon. Planting, business, good luck, good love—there are moon superstitions about almost everything.

• *It is unlucky to see the new moon for the first time through a closed window.*
• *To see a new moon through the branches of a tree will cause bad luck for the entire month.*

- *It is unlucky to see a new moon over your left shoulder, lucky to see it over your right shoulder; and if you see the new moon for the first time straight ahead, you will have happiness for the rest of the season.*
- *You should always show respect for the new moon by bowing to it* THREE *times while turning over silver in your pocket.*
- If you see a new moon and hear a bird call at the same time and then repeat the following CHARM, you will find a HAIR in your right shoe that is the color of your true love's.

> *Bright moon, new moon,*
> *Clear and fair,*
> *Lift up my right foot,*
> *See my love's hair.*

- *Any robbery committed on the third day of a new moon will be quickly discovered.*
- *Anyone who falls ill on the eighth day of the moon is certain to die shortly.*
- *If the full moon shines on your face while you are asleep, you will go crazy.*
- *People are most mad when the moon is full.*
- *The best marriages take place when the moon is full or a few days just before it is full.*
- *A child born at the time of the full moon will always be strong.*
  The "moon line" is the line the moonbeam makes across land or sea.
- *If you cross a moon line as you are going fishing, you will have a poor catch.*
- *Any wish made while someone is crossing the moon line will soon come true.*
- *Two moons in the same month mean bad weather until the next new moon.*

- *If a cresent moon is on its back, with the horns up, it is holding up the rain and a long dry spell can be expected.*
- *A ring around the moon is a sign of rain or snow to come.* You can tell how many days away the storm is by counting the number of stars inside the ring. If there are no stars it will rain within twenty-four hours.
  (See BABY, BIRTH, POINTING, SEVEN)

If LOVERS CROSS *the moon line they will never marry.*

Mop • *To lose a mop overboard is to bring bad luck to the ship.*
• *If you put a mop and a* BROOM *on the doorstep of a new house, they will protect the house from evil spirits until the new owners move in.*
• *When you have finished cleaning,* CROSS *the mop and broom to keep the spirits from making the house dirty right away.*

Moth • *The white moths that fly at night are the souls of the dead.*
• *A white moth flying around someone's head is the spirit of a dead friend.*
• *If a black moth flies into a house someone in the house will die within a year.*

Mouse • *A mouse, roasted, minced, and eaten, will cure a child of measles.*
For best results, the mouse should be roasted live.
• *A roasted mouse will cure colds, sore throats, and fever.*
The roasted mouse cure was used many centuries ago in Egypt, and is still used in parts of Europe and the United States. (See ASTHMA, BED WETTING, WHOOPING COUGH)
• *It is bad luck to see* THREE *mice before dawn.*

Murderer • *A murderer's image remains in the victim's eyes.*
There has long been a belief that the last thing a person sees leaves a permanent picture in the eyes of the CORPSE. (See DIMPLE)

Mushrooms
• *When the* MOON *is at the full,*
Mushrooms you may safely pull.
When the moon is on the wane,
Wait before you pluck again.

Nail • *To get rid of an evil spirit which takes the form of an illness, nail the illness to a* TREE *with an* IRON *nail and then walk away backwards.*
(See HEADACHE)

Name • *It is unlucky to change the name of a horse.*
• *If a child is named after a dead child in the family, the first child will call the living child away.*
• *It brings good luck to have only* SEVEN *letters in either your first or last name.*
• *If you have* THIRTEEN *letters in your name you should add one to change the luck.*
• *Change the name but not the letter,*
  Marry for worse, not for better.
• *To mention the name of a dead person brings bad luck.*
  The use of the name might disturb the person's spirit, which in turn might disturb the living. If the name is mentioned, a phrase such as "May she rest in peace" should be added to stop the spirit from becoming troublesome.
• *When someone is in danger of death, a change of name may confuse the spirits and save the person's life.*
  In some places, a person's real name was kept secret, and other names were used for everyday, so that an enemy could not use the real name to call harm on the person.
• *You can gain power over a god by using the god's true name.*
  The god, however, may become angry. For this reason, people often gave their gods more than one name. The special name was used only in times of great need. (See ABRACADABRA) Jews have long avoided the use of the true name of God, and it is possible that the Commandment

"Thou shalt not take the name of the Lord thy God in vain" was intended to protect people from the anger of God.
(See SHIP)

Napkin • *A guest folding a napkin after a first meal in a house is a sign that the guest will never eat in that house again.*

Needle • *If you break a needle while sewing for yourself you will never live to wear the CLOTHES you are making.*

News • *A BEE buzzing around your head means that good news is coming.*
• *If you split a wooden clothespin in half by accident it means that bad news is on the way.*

New Year's Day • *Empty pockets on New Year's morning are a sign of a poor year to come.*
• *Nothing should be taken out of the house on New Year's Day.*
• *Give a gift on New Year's Day,*
  Give all your luck away.
• *Whatever you are doing on New Year's Day you will do often during the coming year.*
• *The last drink taken from a bottle on New Year's Day will bring good luck to the drinker.*
• *If you eat black-eyed peas on New Year's Day while you have a coin under your plate, and are wearing something RED, you will have good luck all year.*
• *A baby born on New Year's Day will always be lucky.*

New Year's Eve • *Noisemakers should be sounded at midnight of New Year's Eve to scare away the evil spirits.*
In some places the noisemakers are BELLS, in others firecrackers, bamboo sticks, gongs, specially made objects, or just human voices. The source of the NOISE may change, but the superstition is almost universal. Evil spirits have been thought to gather in great numbers at special times of the year, but they are most dangerous at New Year's Eve. At one time the year started in March,

with the coming of spring and in many parts of the world, noise is made at the first new moon in March. Noise should also be made on Midsummer Eve (the day before MIDSUMMER DAY), MAY 1, harvest times, and during all "emergencies" such as droughts, eclipses, and storms.

- *Always open your* WINDOWS *for a few minutes just before midnight on New Year's Eve to let the bad luck out and the good luck in.*
- *It is bad luck to let a fire go out on New Year's Eve.*
- *All debts should be paid and arguments settled before midnight of New Year's Eve.*

Night air • *Night air inside a house is full of poison.* Every door and window should be shut from dusk to dawn to prevent illness. (See DARKNESS)

Nightmare • *To prevent a nightmare, put your socks in the shape of a* CROSS *at the foot of the bed and then place an* IRON *object over the spot where the socks meet.*
- *To prevent a nightmare, hang a* STONE *with a hole in it over the bedpost.*

Nine • Nine is frequently considered a magical number, since it is three times three, and THREE is a special number. Even apart from three, nine seems to possess magic. If you multiply nine by any number, or add nine to nine any number of times, the digits of the product or the sum will always add up to nine or one of its multiples. In India and England, AMULETS were sometimes made of nine STONES or nine KNOTS. Doing something nine times is often part of a CHARM for a cure or for protection from the EVIL EYE. (See STY)

Noise • *Evil spirits can be frightened away by noise.* (See NEW YEAR'S EVE)
• *An unexplained noise in the house that sounds like tearing cloth is a sign of approaching death.*
• *Unexplained* KNOCKS, BELLS, *or raps in the house are signs that illness will soon enter the house.*
(See BREAK, GLASS, KEYS, KNOCK ON WOOD, WHISTLING)

Noodles • In China noodles have long been thought to be a symbol of long life. Noodle dishes are eaten on birthdays and anniversaries to help bring "Many happy returns."

Nosebleed • *To cure a nosebleed, place a silver* KNIFE *just under the nose and press hard while counting to* SEVEN, *seven times.*
(See KEYS)

3·5·7·9

Numbers • *There is more luck in odd numbers than in even numbers.*
Whether they know it or not, even the most sophisticated people have worked the luck of odd numbers into their daily life. Real estate leases, for example, are for ninety-nine years rather than one hundred. And when we want to praise someone, we give THREE cheers. (See NINE, SEVEN, THIRTEEN) Bulgarian and Turkish people often give gifts of money in odd amounts so that the luck of the gift will be good. (See COUNTING, MATCHES, STARS, WEDDING COUPLE)
A LADDER *with an even number of rungs will cause climbers to trip or fall.*

Nurse • *If a nurse knocks over a chair, it is a sign that a new patient will soon arrive.*

Nutmeg • *Nutmeg, carried in a back pocket, is protection against rheumatism.*

Oak tree • *A* NAIL *hammered into an oak tree will cure illness.*
(See HEADACHE, IRON)
• *Flowers bloom on oak trees at midnight of Midsummer Eve,
but the flowers wither and disappear before dawn.*
Midsummer Eve is the day before MIDSUMMER DAY, the
first day of summer.
• *If a person is sick in a house, the house should be warmed
with a fire of oak wood to draw off the illness.*
• *To carve the initials of lovers into an oak tree is to cause the
death of one of the lovers before the year is out.*
Superstitions about oak trees often come from the
Druids, priests of an ancient religion in the land that is
now England. The oak tree was sacred to the Druids,
who believed that the tree had the power to heal and to
bring harm to those who treated it with disrespect.
(See ACORN)

Onion • *Onions should be placed in a sickroom to help
bring health.*
• *An onion cut in half and placed under the bed of a sick person
will draw off fever and poisons.*
• *A slice of onion will stop an insect bite from itching.*
• *An onion worn around the neck from first to last frost will
protect the wearer against colds.* (See GARLIC, WARTS)
• *If you plant onions and potatoes together, neither will grow.*
• *When onions grow with a thick skin
A hard winter is coming in.
When the onion skin is very thin,
A mild winter is coming in.*

Opal • *If you wear an opal, your eyes will become dim or
you will become blind.*
• *Unless you are born in October, it is unlucky to wear opals.*
(See BIRTHSTONE)

Orange blossoms • *To carry orange blossoms on your* WEDDING DAY *will bring good luck.*

The carrying of the blossoms of a fruit tree on a wedding day is a worldwide custom. It asks for double luck—that the TREE spirits bless the couple, and that the bride be fruitful. The type of tree changes with geographical location, but the hope for a happy and fertile marriage remains.

Owl • *It is bad luck to see an owl in the sunlight.*

• *An owl hooting in the early evening is a sign of death.*

To break the curse, kill the owl and bury it near the front door of the house.

Palm Sunday • *If the wind blows from one direction for most of Palm Sunday, it will do so for most of the coming summer.*

Pansies • *To pick pansies in the sunshine is to call the rain.*

Parsley • *Parsley planted on any day but* GOOD FRIDAY *will not grow well.*
• *A gift of parsley will bring bad luck, illness, and even death to the homes of the giver and the receiver.*
Parsley has been associated with death and bad luck since the times when the Romans used it as a decoration around graves.

Peach tree • *If the leaves of a peach tree fall early, there will be illness in the community.*

Peacock feathers • *Peacock feathers in the house will bring bad luck to the family.*
• *A peacock feather in the theater or on stage will bring misfortune to the play or the actors.*

Pearls • *Pearls bring tears except to those born in June.*
• *If you break a string of pearls, the number of pearls left on the string shows the number of times you will cry before the year is out.*
• *A pearl dissolved in vinegar and drunk at the full* MOON *will protect against unlucky changes in life.*
• *Two pearls, left alone in a dark cave underwater, will mate and have a family of new pearls.*
(See BIRTHSTONE)

Peas • *If you find a peapod with ten peas in it, you must eat one and throw the rest of the peas, in the pod, over your right shoulder. Then make a wish and the wish will come true.*

Pencil • *If you use the same pencil to take a test that you used for studying for the test, the pencil will remember the answers.*

• *A new pencil is bad luck in tests.*

Penny • *If you find a heads-up penny, it is especially good luck.*

• *Keeping a jar of pennies in the kitchen will bring good luck.*

• *Pennies should be given along with a sharp-edged gift such as a* KNIFE *or a* SCISSORS *or the friendship will be cut.*
(See COIN, FITS, MONEY)

Pepper • *If you spill pepper you will have a serious argument with your best friend.*

• *People with fever should not eat pepper or the fever will increase.*
(See GUEST)

Photograph • *If* THREE *people are photographed together, the one in the middle will die first.*

• *It is unlucky for an engaged couple to be photographed together.*

• *It is especially bad luck to be photographed with a* CAT.

• *A photograph turned to the wall or put upside down will bring ill luck to the person in the picture.*

• *It is unlucky to be photographed.*
In many places it is thought that people's souls are in their images. To take a photograph is to have control over the soul. (See MIRROR)

Picture • *If a picture falls in the house, someone in the family will die within a month.*

• *A portrait falling is a sign of bad luck to come for the person in the portrait.* (See MIRROR)

Pie • *If you eat the point of a piece of pie before you eat the rest of the piece of pie, you will never marry.*

Pigs • *Pigs can see the wind before it blows near.*
(See FISHING)

Pigeons • *When pigeons gather on the top of a roof, a storm is near.*

Pin

• *See a pin, pick it up*
All the day you'll have good luck.
See a pin, let it lie
All the day you'll have to cry.

• *If you find a pin pointed toward you, it is a sign that you have a new and dangerous enemy.*

• *Lend a pin, spoil a friendship.*
If someone asks you for a pin, say "Take it, I won't lend it." The person should pick up the pin from wherever it lays without saying thank you.

• *A pin should never be used to take out a splinter.*
If a pin, instead of a needle, is used to take out a splinter, the wound will take a long time to heal.
(See CANDLE, ENEMY, KNIFE, WARTS)

Play • *To give the last line of a play during dress rehearsal will bring bad luck to the play.*
(See LUCK, PEACOCK FEATHERS, STAGE, WHISTLING)

Playing cards • *It is bad luck to drop a single card on the floor while playing cards.*
• SINGING *while you play cards will bring bad luck.*

Pointing • *To point at a ship will bring bad luck to the ship and to all aboard.*
• *It is bad luck to point at the* MOON.
• *It is bad luck to point at people. The bad luck will fall on the one who points and the one pointed at.*
Curses were supposed to be called into being by pointing at a person while saying a CHARM. People with the EVIL EYE were often thought to point at their victims. In the United States and much of Europe, pointing is considered bad manners, if not bad luck. (See GRAVES)

Poker • *If you put the poker and the tongs on the same side of the fireplace, there will soon be a quarrel in the house.*
• *A fire can be made to burn better by placing the poker upright against the grate.*

Potato • *When the new potatoes are dug, all who help with the digging and everyone in their families must taste the potatoes or the crop will be insulted and rot quickly.*
(See CROPS, ONIONS, RHEUMATISM)

Poultry • *Just before a farmer's death, all his poultry goes to roost at noon instead of dusk.*
(See ROOSTER)

Prayer • *The Lord's Prayer said backwards will protect against evil.*
(See HICCUPS, WITCHES)

Praying mantis • *It is very bad luck to kill a praying mantis.*
• *There is a twenty-five-dollar fine for harming a praying mantis.*

Pregnancy • *If a diaper is left in a house by a visiting mother, the woman of the house will soon become pregnant.*

• *A woman who lends her maternity* CLOTHES *will soon become pregnant again.*

• *Great danger will come to a pregnant woman who crosses a stream.*

• *A pregnant woman should never try to can fruit because the fruit is sure to spoil.*

• *An unborn child that is "carried high" is a girl, one that is "carried low" is a boy.*

• To make sure her unborn child is a boy, a pregnant woman should sleep with a knife in the mattress; to make sure the child is a girl, she should put a frying pan under the bed.

• *A pregnant woman should satisfy any craving for a certain food or the child will be born with a birthmark in the shape of the food.*

• *Children are marked by what their mothers see, hear, and do during pregnancy.*
(See CRADLE, JADE)

Pumpkin • *It is bad luck to sleep in a room with a pumpkin.*

Puppies • *It you bury* THREE *puppies from the same litter in a field, weeds will never grow there.*

109

Quarrel • *The husband should always be the one to lock the front door for the night.*
If the wife locks up, there will be a quarrel the next day.
• *If two people are talking together and a third person comes between them, they must turn away from the third at once.*
Turning away is not an insult to the third person; it is done to prevent a quarrel between the first two.
• *If food or drink is given in a plate or container which is to be returned, the plate or container must not be returned empty or there will soon be a quarrel.*
• *Borrowing yeast or salt is borrowing a quarrel.*
• *If you borrow or give a PIN you will soon quarrel with a friend.*

• *You must always leave a neighbor's house by the same door you entered or you will cause a serious quarrel.*
(See BREAD AND BUTTER, HANDS, KISS, KNIFE, PEPPER, POKER, TOWEL)

Quilt • *A quilt should always be mended by darning, never by patching. A patched quilt will give a poor rest.*
• *Quilts should always be washed in snow water to give a gentle rest to the spirits of those who made the quilt.*
(See DREAM)

Rabbit • The hare, an animal much like a rabbit, was worshipped in parts of what is now England before the Christian conversion. The new church outlawed the old religion but beliefs about hares continued and were later broadened to include rabbits. (See MISTLETOE) Since rabbits are more common than hares, most of the superstitions name rabbits. The luck of the rabbit stems from the fact that rabbits are born with their eyes open. They have power over the EVIL EYE, since they can see evil at once and send it away.

• *The hind foot of a rabbit, carried in your LEFT pocket, will bring good luck.*
For best luck the rabbit should have been killed at a crossroad when the MOON was full.

• *If a rabbit runs along a road in front of a house, the house will catch on fire during the day.*

• *Witches sometimes take the form of rabbits.*
• *A child brushed at birth with a rabbit's hind foot will always be lucky.*
• *If a rabbit's hind foot is placed in a child's crib and carriage, while the child is out of them, no harm will come to the child.*
• *A rabbit's hind foot should always be used by actors and actresses to put on rouge, and when not in use should be kept in the makeup box.*
Loss of the rabbit's foot will bring loss of talent.

• *Tea made from the dried droppings of wild male rabbits will cure fever when drunk every half-hour until sweating starts.*
(See FEBRUARY 14, WHITE RABBIT)

Races • *If a* PHOTOGRAPH *is taken of jockey and horse together before a race, they will lose the race.*
• *A jockey's boots should never be put on the floor before they are put on or the jockey will be slow.*
(See GOLF)

Rain • *If you burn ferns you will bring rain.*
• *It will rain if you water the lawn.*
• *Rain caught and saved on Holy Thursday is a sure cure for sore eyes.*
• *Rain at a funeral is a sign that the spirit has gone to heaven.*
• *If you stand in the first rain that falls in May, you will be healthy until the first snowfall.*
• *Rain falling on your head will make your* HAIR *grow faster.*
(See CAR, HORSE, JADE, MOON, PANSIES, RAINBOW, WEATHER)

Rainbow • *If you dig where the end of the rainbow touches the ground you will find a pot of gold.*
• *A rainbow on Saturday is a sign of rain in the coming week.*
• *A rainbow in the morning means a storm; a rainbow at night means fair weather.*
• *A rainbow during rain means the* SUN *will soon shine.*
• *A rainbow is the bridge over which souls are taken away.*
To keep the soul on earth, CROSS out the rainbow by making crosses on the ground with a willow stick.

Rainwater • *If a baby's first bath is in rainwater, the baby will talk early and never stutter.*
• *Money washed in rainwater cannot be stolen.*

Rats • *If rats suddenly leave a ship or a house there will soon be death or disaster.*
• *A rat's tail, dried and powdered, will cure* TOOTHACHE.
Superstition connects rats and teeth in many parts of the world because rats' teeth are so strong. A common superstition is one in which a child's milk tooth is thrown into the grass where rats nest with a CHARM asking the

rats to accept the tooth and to give a strong one in return.

• To get rid of rats in a house, barn, or field, write the following charm on a piece of paper and place the paper where the rats can find it.

**RATS
ARST
TSRA
STAR**

It is widely believed that rats can read, and in many places letters are written to ask them to leave and to suggest places where they would be happier.

Raven • *To kill a raven is to harm the spirit of King Arthur, who visits the world in the form of a raven.*
(See BIRDS)

Red • Red is often thought to be a special and protective color and is used in many CHARMS. (See BLUE, KNOTS)

• *A red ribbon should be placed on a child who has been sick to help keep the illness from returning.*
• *A red string tied around a* FINGER *on the* LEFT *hand is an aid to good memory.*
• *A red string worn around the neck will prevent rheumatism.*
• *A red ribbon should be placed on a newborn child or on its crib before the baby is shown to people outside the family for the first time.*

The ribbon will protect the child from the EVIL EYE. An outgrowth of red ribbons on a crib is the modern practice of using colored balls as decoration on infants' furniture.

Red hair • *Red* HAIR *is a sign of bad temper.*
• *It is lucky to see a red-haired girl on a* WHITE HORSE.

It is lucky to see a red-haired girl on a white horse.

Rheumatism • *A potato which has been stolen or begged will protect against rheumatism.*

• *A silver* RING *from a used coffin hinge will both prevent and cure rheumatism.*

(See BEES, COPPER, NUTMEG, RED, WEATHER)

Rhyme • If you make a rhyme by accident, you will soon see a loved one.

• *Make a rhyme, make a rhyme,*
See your love before bedtime.

Rice • *Throwing rice at a newly married couple will help ensure their fruitfulness.*

The practice of throwing rice at a newly married couple is almost worldwide, but most likely started in the Orient where life may depend on a good rice crop. In ancient Rome wheat, the most important crop, was thrown at the newlyweds. Fruits, especially figs, were used in parts of southern Europe.

Right • *Good spirits live on the right side of the body, bad spirits on the* LEFT.

• *All turns should be to the right for luck.*

The right turn is in the direction in which the SUN moves, the left is the direction of evil.

Rings • Rings were first worn for protection against evil and illness, not for decoration. It was thought that no evil could get past the CIRCLE and into the body. In early times the rings may have been associated with the circles witches and magicians drew around themselves for protection while calling the spirits to do their bidding. Rings are also thought to tie people together. Not only married couples, but friends, kings and their most faithful servants, gods and their followers, have exchanged rings as a symbol of their vows. It was thought that if the rings were removed, the ties that bound the people would be loosened. The binding power of rings was thought to be so strong that in some places rings were removed from the fingers of dying people for fear that their souls would otherwise not be able to go free. (See CRAMP, FINGER, FITS, GOOD FRIDAY, HORSESHOE, RHEUMATISM, WEDDING BAND)

Robin

- *If a robin you should dare to kill,*
  Your right hand will lose all its skill.
- *If a* CAT *catches and kills a robin the cat will soon lose a leg.*
- *A wish made upon seeing the first robin in spring will come true.*
- *A robin redbreast in a cage*
  Sets all heaven in a rage.

The robin is thought by many to be a special bird. Traditional stories say that the robin got its red breast when it pulled the thorns out of the crown of Jesus. Even earlier stories say that the bird got its red breast from carrying water in its beak to a good king caught in a fire of the devil. The bird went too close to the fire and its breast feathers burned. (See HOLLY, WINDOW, WITCH)

Rooster

- *If a rooster crows while going to bed,*
  He'll wake up with a wet head.
- *If a rooster crows near a door, with his head toward it, a stranger is coming to the house.*
- *When a rooster crows at midnight it is a sign to all spirits to return to the other world.*

Rosemary • *Rosemary, worn in a cotton bag around the neck, will give a good memory.*
- *Rosemary planted at the doorstep will keep witches away.*
  The following CHARM is sometimes said while rosemary is being planted:

> *Run witch run, flee witch flee,*
> *Or it will go ill with thee.*
> *Run witch flee. Begone!*

Roses • *Roses blooming beyond the season foretell* DEATH *from disease in the coming year for a member of the family.*

Rowan wood • Rowan wood (mountain ash) is a strong AMULET against the EVIL EYE and certain bad spirits. Superstitions about rowan wood are common in northern Europe and in parts of the United States, but they were probably originally Greek. A piece of forked rowan wood is thought to be especially lucky. The wood must never be cut with IRON.

• *Rowan tree and* RED *thread*
Hold the witches still in dread.

Rust • *If an object made of* IRON *or steel rusts when you have taken good care of it, it is a sign that money is being saved for you.*

S

Sage • *To ensure a long life, eat sage in* MAY.

Sailor • *Touch a sailor's collar for luck.*
(See ALBATROSS, DROWNING, GLASS, GOOD FRIDAY, TATTOO)

St. Mark's Eve • *If you stand in a cemetery on St. Mark's Eve (April 24), you will see the ghosts of those who are to die in the coming year.*

St. Swithin's Day • *If it rains on St. Swithin's Day (July 15), it will do so for forty days.*
As a monk, St. Swithin always liked being outside in the fields. When he died in England in 862 A.D., he asked to be buried outside, and was. Many years later he was made a saint, and the monks decided he would be more honored if his coffin were moved inside the church. On the day that they planned to make the move, it started to rain and the rain continued for forty days—until the monks agreed to leave St. Swithin outside.

Salt • Salt is necessary to life, but throughout history in much of the world salt has been expensive and difficult to get. The value of salt is shown in the many superstitions about it. Early Jews honored salt because the numerical value of its letters is the same as that of one of the most holy NAMES of God.
• *Bad luck will follow the spilling of salt unless a pinch of it is thrown over the* LEFT *shoulder into the face of the devil waiting there.*
• *Salt should never be passed from one person's hand to another's at the table.*
Salt should be put down on the table before being picked up, or bad luck will follow both people. The chance of spilling salt is greater if salt is passed from hand to hand.

- *To salt another person's food or to put salt on that person's plate is to bring bad luck to yourself and the other person.*
- *Help to salt, help to sorrow.*
- *Put salt on the doorstep of a new house and no evil can enter.*
- *Carry a teaspoon full of salt in a small cloth bag in your suitcase to keep safe from danger when you travel.*
- *You can catch a bird by putting salt on its tail.*
- *Salty soup is a sign that the cook is in love.*

Saturday • *A new* MOON *on Saturday brings bad luck.*
- *The* SUN *shines on every Saturday of the year, even if only for a minute.*

Scissors • *It is unlucky to pick up a pair of scissors which you have dropped. Always have someone else do it for you.* If there is no one to pick up the scissors for you, you can stop the bad luck by blowing on the scissors before touching them and then warming them in your hand before using them. The danger, and the power, of scissors comes from the IRON of which they were originally made.
- *Scissors should never be accepted as a gift without giving a* PENNY *in return.*
(See KNIFE, WITCHES)

Sea gull • *It is unlucky to kill a sea gull.*
In many primitive seaside communities, this is not a superstition as much as it is a health measure. Sea gulls are scavengers; they eat dead fish and other things which might spread disease if left on the beach. In parts of England, however, it is believed that sea gulls are the souls of the dead.
- *Three sea gulls flying together, directly overhead, are a warning of death soon to come.*

Seal • *If you kill a seal, someone in your family will drown.*

Seawater • *If the first thing you eat or drink each morning is seawater, you will live forever.*

Seaweed • *Dried seaweed, kept on the mantel piece, will keep the house from catching fire.*

Seeds • *Seeds that are planted on the last* THREE *days of March will not grow.*
(See APPLE)

Seven • Seven is thought to be a special number. It is believed by many people that the body and mind of every person completely changes over a seven-year period. The belief may come from the phases of the MOON, which change every seven days.
- *The seventh of anything brings good luck.*
- *If you keep an unnecessary object for seven years you will find a use for it.*
- *A seventh son can cure diseases.*
The seventh son of a seventh son is a doctor who needs no training.

Shadow • *You will have good luck if you step on your own shadow, but it is bad luck if someone else steps on it.*

Shaking hands • *Shaking hands to complete a deal or to greet someone brings good luck.*
The good luck comes because the hands of the two people form a CROSS. Handshaking to show agreement is an early "crossing" custom.

Sheep • *If the first lambs born in a flock are white twins, there will be a great increase in the number of sheep in the flock.*

Shingles • Shingles is a disease which causes painful sores in different places on the body. In some cases, the sores start around the back of the waist and move, on either side, toward the front of the body. It is believed by some that if the sores ever go completely around the body the patient will die at once.

Ship • *To change the* NAME *of a ship is to invite disaster.*

• *A hatch cover turned upside down on a ship will bring bad luck.*
The upside-down hatch cover is thought to be a sign that the ship itself will be turned upside down.
(See ALBATROSS, BODY, MOP, WHISTLING)

Shoelace • *If your shoelace comes untied, your true love is thinking of you.*

Shoes • *Throwing a shoe after a bride will bring her husband good luck.*

• *It is bad luck to accidentally* CROSS *your shoes when you are not wearing them.*
To stop the bad luck, get another person to uncross them.

• *Shoes put on a table are a sign that death will soon come to the house.*

• *It brings bad luck to walk even one step with one shoe on and one shoe off. You will have a year of tears for each step you take.*

• *It is bad luck to put your* LEFT *shoe on first.*

• *Wear your shoes out at the toe,*
Lose your money as you go,
Wear your shoes out at the side,
You will marry a rich bride,
Wear your shoes out at the heel,
You will soon spend a good deal,
Wear your shoes out on the ball,
You will live to spend it all.
(See LOVERS)

Shooting stars • *All wishes on shooting stars come true.*

• *If you do not wish on a shooting star when you see one you will be unlucky all year.*

• *Shooting stars mean that someone is about to die.*
The stars mark a path to heaven for the soul. To make sure that the shooting star is not marking a path for anyone in your family, say very quickly "Not from my family" THREE times.
(See STARS)

Silence • *Sudden silences usually occur at twenty minutes before or after the hour.*

• *Sudden silence in a room means that someone has died.*
Silence is connected with death. Even today we observe moments of silence for those who have died.

Singing

• *Sing before breakfast,*
Cry before night.

• *Sing while eating*
Or sing in bed,
Evil will get you
And you'll be dead.

(See PLAYING CARDS, SWAN, URINATION)

Skull • *If you tell a lie while swearing on a skull, you will die at once.*

Sleep • *The best sleep is sleep on the RIGHT side.*

• *You sleep best with your head to the north and your feet to the south.*
Some people believe that magnetic waves flow from the North Pole to the South Pole and if you sleep against the waves you will not rest easy.
(See MOON, PUMPKIN)

Sleepwalkers • *If you awaken a sleepwalker suddenly it may cause that person's death.*

Snail • To discover the initials of your true love's name, take a snail and put it on a flour-covered board and then put a large glass bowl over it. In the morning you will find your love's initials in the trail of the snail.

Snake • *No matter how many pieces it is cut in to, a snake will never die when the sun is out.*

• *If you eat snake you will never grow old.*
(See HEADACHE, YOUTH)

Sneeze • *A newborn child is under the spell of elves until it sneezes.*

• *If you sneeze while telling a LIE it will become the truth.*

• *Sneeze on Monday, sneeze for danger;*
Sneeze on Tuesday, kiss a stranger;
Sneeze on Wednesday, get a letter;
Sneeze on Thursday, something better;
Sneeze on Friday, sneeze for sorrow;
Sneeze on Saturday, see your lover tomorrow.

(See SUNDAY)

• *Say "God bless you," "Good health," or other CHARMS to keep people safe from harm after they sneeze.*
It was once believed that people held their lives in their breath. A sneeze might let the life out of a person. A sneeze might also leave a space in the head that could be lived in by evil spirits. In some places, instead of saying a charm, hands were clapped to scare the spirits off and to chase life back into the person. (See CEMETERY, YAWN)

Snow • *The number of times it snows in the winter is the same as the number of fogs the previous August.*
(See MOON, SOOT)

Soap • *It is unlucky to have soap slip out of your hands.*

Socks • *Dark-colored socks with white toes protect the wearer from being tripped by elves.*
• *To bring good luck during the day, the* LEFT *sock should be put on first.*
• *It is tempting fate to walk with socks on and no shoes.* Some Jews do not wear shoes at home during the period of mourning and it may be from this practice that the superstition stems.

Solomon's seal • Solomon's seal is an AMULET against fever made of two intertwined TRIANGLES which form a six-pointed STAR. The seal is also known as the star of David.

Soot • *If the soot on the outside bottom of a pot burns, there will soon be snow.*

Sparrow • *It is unlucky to kill a sparrow.*
• *Sparrows carry the souls of the dead.*

Spider • *To kill a spider brings bad luck.*
• *If you find a spider on your clothes you will soon receive money. If someone else finds a spider on your clothes you will soon lose money.*
• *A spider in the morning is a sign of sorrow;*
A spider at noon brings worry for tomorrow;
A spider in the afternoon is a sign of a gift;
But a spider in the evening will all hopes uplift.

(See COBWEB, JAUNDICE)

Spit • Spit, or saliva, is one of the fluids of the body and has been thought to be important everywhere in the world. Jesus was said to have cured blindness using clay made of dirt and spit. It has often been used to protect against evil, to bring good luck, or to cure. The Masai people, in what is now Tanzania, believed that spitting was a sign of goodwill. They spat at each other to say hello and goodby and to seal bargains. In Ireland people spit on a newborn baby to bring the baby luck. In the Sandwich Islands, chiefs were once followed by servants carrying spittoons. It was thought an enemy who got any of the chief's saliva could work spells against the chief. (See BOILS, EYELASHES, FINGERNAILS, HAIR)

• *Spit on the ground in the presence of evil to halt the evil.*
• *If you spit loudly* THREE *times when you are frightened, no harm will come to you.* (See NOISE)
• *Spit on your hands for luck before you fight.*
• *Spit into a boat before sailing to ensure good winds.* (See BASEBALL, COIN)

Spoon • *It brings bad luck in cooking to pour gravy backhanded out of a spoon.*
• *Two spoons in a saucer are a sign that a wedding is soon to come.*

Sprain • A sprain can be cured by wrapping a piece of RED WOOL SEVEN times around the injured limb and saying,

> *Bone to bone,*
> *Vein to vein,*
> *Become whole*
> *And rest again.*

Spring cleaning • *All spring cleaning must be finished before May begins or the cleaning will go to waste.*

Square of Saturn • The Square of Saturn is a MAGIC
SQUARE, devised to help the user control luck. In Hebrew
each letter also stands for a number. In the Square of
Saturn each row, in every direction, adds up to fifteen.
It has been believed that if you want to control fate or the
acts of another person, you can form this square on a
piece of paper, make your wish, and burn the paper.
Your wish will soon come true. (See ABRACADABRA)

Stage • *An actor who stumbles as he walks on stage will
miss a cue during the evening.*
• Macbeth *is an unlucky play to put on stage because the
Witches' Song can raise evil.*
• *Real flowers should not be worn on stage.*
• *If you look over your shoulder into a* MIRROR *while on stage
you will cause terrible misfortune to occur.*
(See KNIT, PLAY)

Stairs • *It is unlucky to meet and pass anyone on the stairs.*
(See BIRTH, STONE STEPS, TRIP)

Stars • Stars have long been considered lucky symbols.
(See WISHES) We call our most famous people "stars"
and the star is used by more nations on their flag than
any other symbol—over forty nations use it in one form
or another. (See TOTEM) "Mazel tov," the Hebrew way of
saying "Good luck," really means "Good constellation"
or "May the stars be good to you." (See GLASS)
• *The stars that fall from heaven are the souls of children
coming to earth to be born.* (See SHOOTING STARS)
• *It is bad luck to count more than* THIRTEEN *stars.*
• *If you try to count one hundred stars you will die as you
count the last one.* (See NUMBERS)

Stealing • *If you carry a toad's heart in your pocket you can steal without being found out.*
(See MOON, THIEF)

Stitch in the side • *To cure a stitch in your side, find a dark-colored flat* STONE, *rub the stitch with it,* SPIT *on the stone, and put it back exactly where you found it.*

Stones • Stones which are very different from those generally found in an area are often thought to be special—perhaps even to have come from the spirits. (See STITCH IN THE SIDE) Stones with natural holes through them are thought to have special powers of healing and are often used as AMULETS. In some places very large stones with holes through them were placed in the middle of a field. If a sick person was passed through the hole at high noon or during certain phases of the MOON, the illness was supposed to be cured. Small stones with holes in them should never be put in pockets or other dark places. Instead, they should be strung on a cord to hold the luck in them, and hung on a person or a building.

Stone steps • *Sitting on stone steps will make you hardhearted.*

Stork • *A stork brings many children and good luck to the family living in the house where it makes its nest.*

Storms • *If you cut your* HAIR *or nails at sea while the sea is calm, you will cause a fierce storm.*
(See PIGEONS*)*

Sty • *To cure a sty in your eye rub the sty* NINE *times with a gold* WEDDING BAND.

• *To cure a sty, pull one* HAIR *from the tail of a* BLACK CAT *on the first night of the new* MOON *and rub the top of the hair nine times over the sty.*

Sun • *The sun hides before great sorrow.*
Many countries have such superstitions. It is most likely that they come from the fear of solar eclipses.
• *Born at sunrise, born clever;*
Born at sunset, born lazy.
(See CIRCLE, EASTER)

Sunday • *If you* SNEEZE *on Sunday morning without any reason before you have eaten anything, you will be lucky in love forever.*
• *It is good luck to be born on Sunday.* (See BIRTH)
• *A fever is always worse on Sunday. If it gets better on Sunday, the illness will soon return.*

Sunrise • *There are more deaths at sunrise than at any other time.*
This belief, and the practice of killing condemned persons at sunrise, may date back to the worship of the SUN. In almost every culture, sacrifices to the sun have been made at sunrise.
Many CHARMS are not effective unless worked before or at sunrise. (See FRECKLES, MAY 1, THURSDAY)

Swallow • *To pull down a swallow's nest from your house is to pull down your luck.*
• *It is a sign of luck in the coming year for a swallow to build a nest on your house. But if the swallow starts to build and then deserts the nest, it is a sign of death to come.*
• *Every swallow has three drops of the blood of a person who became an angel.*
Swallows are often thought to be sacred, or at least lucky, because they are usually the first birds to return each spring.

Swan • *All swans are hatched during thunderstorms.*
• *Swans sing sweetly just before death.*

Sweeping • *All sweeping should be done from the sides of the house toward the middle. Dust should be carried out of the house.*

• *If you sweep dust out of your house you will sweep away all good fortune.*

In some places it is believed that spirits gather outside the door of houses and if you sweep the dust out the door you will be throwing dust on them. There are superstitions about sweeping and BROOMS in every type of culture; this is one of the most common.

• *If you sweep on Monday you will sweep your money away.*

• *Sweep after dark,*
Bring sorrow to your heart.

(See BED)

Swimming • *It is unhealthy to swim between July 3 and August 11.*

This period of time is called the "dog days" and has been thought to be unhealthy since ancient times. Flies increase, rain seldom falls, and, supposedly, dogs go mad and snakes go blind and strike at any sound.

Table • *If you sit on a table while talking to your sweetheart,*
you will never marry each other.
(See SHOE, THIRTEEN)

Talisman • A talisman is an object which, like an AMULET,
brings good luck to the user. Talismans often contain
mystical signs, pictures, words, and letters. Unlike
an amulet the talisman cannot protect against evil.

Talk • *If you talk when passing under a railway BRIDGE,*
you will call bad luck your way.

• *Speak of a person,*
And he will appear;
Then talk of the devil,
And he will draw near.

(See ANIMALS)

Tattoo • *A tattoo will protect a sailor from drowning and the pox.*

Tea • *If you put milk or cream into tea before you put in the*
sugar, you will lose your lover.
• *It is bad luck for two people to pour tea from the same pot.*
• *A tea leaf floating in a cup of tea means that a stranger will*
soon come to visit.
To tell exactly when the visitor is coming, take the tea
leaf out of the cup and put it on the back of your LEFT
hand. Tap the tea leaf with the little finger of your right
hand. The number of taps it takes until the leaf falls off
your hand is the number of days that will pass until the
stranger comes.
• *If you stir tea leaves in the teapot, you will stir trouble into*
your life.

Teeth • *It is luckier to have the baby's first tooth in the lower jaw than in the upper.*
• *Front teeth set wide apart are a sign that a person is lucky in love and will travel.*
• *A child's milk teeth should be carefully saved so that they are not used by an enemy to cause bodily harm.*
(See EYELASHES, FINGERNAILS, HAIR, SPIT)
• *There will be less pain and better healing if a tooth is pulled in the morning than if it is pulled in the afternoon.*
(See RATS, TOOTHACHE)

Tennis • *If you hold* THREE *balls in your hand while you are serving at tennis, you will have bad luck at the game.*
(See GOLF)

Thief • *A thief always looks into a cup before drinking.*
(See BABY, STEALING)

Thirteen • Although it is often said that thirteen became an unlucky number because there were thirteen people at the Last Supper, the number was considered unlucky long before that. In ancient Norse mythology there was also a supper after which thirteen was said to become unlucky. Twelve gods were invited to a supper. After they had arrived, Loki, the spirit of mischief, arrived without being invited. At the supper, one of the gods was killed. It is most likely, however, that the fear of the number thirteen goes back even further than Loki. In very early times people counted to ten on their fingers. Then they added each hand to get twelve. Anything over twelve was unknown and therefore unlucky. Some peoples, however, having seen that there were thirteen moons in a year, thought the number to be lucky.
• *If thirteen people sit down at a table to eat, one of them will die before the year is over.*

The only way to stop the death is for everyone to stand at the same time at the end of the meal, all holding hands. In this way the people will all be bound together as a single unit instead of thirteen separate units.

- *A happy life cannot be lived in a house numbered thirteen.* In France there are no houses numbered thirteen, and in the United States and many other countries skyscrapers have no floor numbered thirteen.

Three • Three has been considered a special number since early times. Most likely it stemmed from the birth of a child, which results in the sacred three: a man, a woman, a child. Without this three there could be no continuation of life. The Trinity of Christianity, and of other earlier religions, may be connected to the importance of three. Three has also been thought to symbolize birth, life, and death or the beginning, the middle, and the end. (See TRIANGLE)

- *Good and bad things come in threes.* (See CIGARETTES)
- *If there is one accident there will soon be two more.*
- To protect against the evil that may come from breaking a superstition, say the following charm of three, completing the necessary action:

> *I turn myself three times about*
> *And put all evil luck to rout.*

There are many superstitions in which CHARMS must be repeated three times or in multiples of three. (See NINE) Three shots are still fired over the grave of a military person as the coffin is lowered into the grave. We are still given three chances, three wishes, and three cheers, and in baseball we get three strikes.

Thunder • *If thunder is heard between November 30 and January 31, the most important person within hearing will die.*
• *Thunderstorms can be kept away by ringing church bells.*
• *Thunderstorms can be called into an area by beating on bronze gongs.*
• *Thunder can kill young birds in their nest.*
• *To say the word "thunder" during a thunderstorm is to call the danger to yourself.*
• *Thunder and lightning can make milk go sour unless a rusty* NAIL *is put in the milk.*
• *Thunder on the right hand,*
Thunder for ill.
Thunder on the LEFT *hand*
Shows goodwill.

(See ACORN, SWAN, TURTLE)

Thursday • *Thursday is an unlucky day with only one lucky hour, the hour before* SUNRISE.

Tickle • *If you tickle a baby's toe before it is* THREE *months old, it will stammer when it talks.*

Toad • *If you kill a toad, the water in the community will go bad.*
(See EVIL EYE, STEALING, WARTS)

Toes • *If your second toe is longer than your big toe, you will be a bully.*
• *Stub your toe,*
Kiss your thumb,
You'll see your beau
'Fore bedtime comes.

Tongue • *If you bite your tongue while eating, it is because you have recently told a lie.*
• *If you never touch the hole that a tooth came out of with your tongue, the new tooth will grow in pure gold.*
(See EARS)

Toothache • *A* NAIL *pounded into an* OAK TREE *will cure a toothache.* (See IRON)

- *If you always put your right leg into your socks first, your right leg into your pants first, and your right foot into your shoe first, you will never have a toothache.*
  (See ABRACADABRA, RATS)

Totem • A totem is a natural object, such as an animal, bird, plant, or star, which is taken as a symbol by a group of people. The totem is thought to bring luck to the group and to pass on to the group its characteristics. A group with the totem of a wolf, for example, will expect the totem to help make it fierce, while a group with a totem of a bird will expect to be swift and far-moving.

Towel • *If two people use the same towel at the same time, there will be a quarrel.*
- *Wash and dry together, Soon you'll cry together.*
  If you do use a towel with someone by mistake, you can take the bad luck out of the act by twisting the towel THREE times between yourselves.

Tracks • *If anyone walks directly in your tracks in snow or mud, or if you walk in anyone else's, you will have headaches or even go blind.*

Tree • In many parts of the world, trees, which are so necessary to life, were thought to be sacred or to hold both good and evil spirits. (See KNOCK ON WOOD) Cures were often thought to be accomplished by nailing the disease to a tree. (See HEADACHE, IRON, NAIL, OAK TREE) The evil spirit of the disease was supposed to be overcome by the good spirits of the tree.
- In Germany a cold could be cured by walking around the biggest tree within sight THREE times at SUNRISE while saying

  Good morning tree, both good and old, I bring thee the warm and the cold.

- In parts of southern India, some people believed that a tree marriage should take place at the same time as a regular wedding. Any evil that might go to the human BRIDE and groom was supposed to go to the tree bride and groom.
- In many countries, trees have been planted at the birth of a child, with the hope that the tree spirits would protect the child. The tree could not be cut down without causing harm to the child.
  (See MOON)

Triangle • Because it has THREE sides and is one of the strongest physical structures that can be built, a triangle is often considered a sacred form. (See ABRACADABRA, MAGIC SQUARE) To walk under a LADDER which is leaning against a wall breaks a triangle and so brings bad luck.
- *Three NAILS, in the form of a triangle, driven into the front door, will protect a house from witches. (See IRON)*

Trip • *It is good luck to trip into your own home.*
- *To trip going upstairs is a sign that there will soon be a wedding in the house. If, however, that same night you dream of a horse, there will be a death instead.*
  (See BRIDE, NUMBERS)

Turtle • *If a turtle bites you it will not let go until it hears a clap of thunder.*

Two-dollar bill • *A two-dollar bill is unlucky.*
  To take the bad luck off a two-dollar bill, tear one corner off so that the bill has THREE corners. The luck of three will then protect the bill. If you kiss the bill or SPIT on it, the luck will also change from bad to good.

Typing • *If the lines come out even on the right side of the paper when you are typing the final copy of something you have written, you have created a masterpiece.*

Umbilical cord • *The umbilical cord carries part of the soul of the child.*
In many places it is believed that the umbilical cord should either be burned or made into an AMULET. If disposed of in any other way it could fall into the hands of the devil or an evil spirit and be used to cause trouble for the child. (See EYELASHES, FINGERNAILS, HAIR, SPIT)

Umbrella • *To open an umbrella in the house will bring bad luck.*
In parts of the Asian world, as early as the eleventh century B.C., umbrellas were used to protect people from the rays of the SUN. It was considered an insult to the sun to raise an umbrella in the shade, and especially inside a building.
• *If you drop an umbrella, and pick it up yourself, you will have bad luck.*
Urination • *It is unlucky to sing or whistle while urinating.*

Valentine's Day • It is considered lucky to send and receive messages of love on this day. (See FEBRUARY 14)

Veil • Brides once wore veils to protect themselves from the EVIL EYE. Evil spirits never like to see people happy and are supposed to hate weddings most of all. A veil disguises the bride and confuses the evil spirits.

Vein • *A* BLUE *vein on the bridge of your nose is a sign that you will lead a happy but short life.*

Vertigo • *To cure vertigo, go out at dawn on the first of May and sniff the dew from the grass.*

Violence • *To protect yourself against violence, wear a* STONE *with a hole through it on a* RED *thread around your neck.*

Visitor
• *A name that is spoken before breakfast is eaten,*
  Will be used before dinner as a glad greeting.
  (See CHOPSTICKS, FORK, GUEST, ITCH, TEA)

V sign • *If you make a V sign with the forefinger and the middle finger of your right hand, with the fingers* POINTING *down, as your first act each morning, the devil will not be able to get near you.*
The V sign represents the devil and his horns. When you point the V sign down, you are forcing the devil to stay below where he belongs.

Warts • *To cure a wart steal a piece of meat, rub it on the wart, and bury it. As the meat rots away, the wart will disappear.*

• When a funeral passes, rub your warts and say

> *As this body goes its way*
> *Let these warts pass away.*

The warts will be gone by the time it has rained NINE times.

• *Tie a* RED *thread around a wart, wrapping it* THREE *times.*

• *Unwrap the thread and bury it in the ground where no one will find it.*

After NINE days the wart will start to disappear.

• You can pass a wart to someone else by paying a PENNY to the other person for each wart. The penny has to have a hole in it and the exchange has to be made in a cemetery at midnight.

• *Put as many pebbles as you have warts in a small paper bag. Walk down the right side of the street alone and throw the bag over your right shoulder.*

The person who picks up the bag and counts the pebbles will get your warts.

• *Touch a wart with nine beans and throw the beans over your right shoulder without ever turning around or looking to see where the beans fall.*

As the beans rot, so will the wart. Some people use the same charm with nine slices from different ONIONS instead of the beans. In about 50 A.D., the Romans believed that the wart should be touched with a chick-pea on the first day of the new MOON. The chick-pea was then wrapped in cloth and thrown away over the right shoulder.

- *Cut an apple in half and rub each wart with each part of the apple. Fasten the apple together and bury it.*
  As the apple rots it will take the warts with it.
- *Take a never-used pin and* CROSS *each wart with it nine times. Throw the pin away over your* LEFT *shoulder without looking back.*
  The person who picks up the pin and uses it will get your warts. Some people say that the wart must be crossed with the pin through a golden WEDDING BAND. *You can get warts from touching toads.*
  (See EGGS, KNOTS)

Washing • *If you splatter water while washing your* HANDS *in the morning, you will ruin your luck for the day.*

Wasps • *If you kill the first wasp you see each year, you will always win over your enemies.*

Water • *Water which is taken from a running stream or creek at midnight on Easter will turn into wine.*
- *Water taken from* THREE *separate streams before* SUNRISE, *in silence, on Sunday morning and then mixed in an earthenware jar becomes magic water which can be used to cure eye and skin diseases.*
- *Hot water will freeze faster than cold water.*
- *Boiled water should never be left in a bedroom overnight.*
  It was once believed that boiled water could not freeze and that if it were left in a bedroom overnight the devil might try to freeze it, become angry because he could not, and do harm to the person in the room.
  (See RAINWATER, SEAWATER, WASHING, WAVES, WINDOWSILL)

Waves • *To cure a high and long-lasting fever, catch the tops of* NINE *waves in a jar.*
  Use the water to wash the face of the patient by putting the water on and wiping it off in the direction of the SUN.

Weather • *The weather for each season is determined by the weather of the first three days of the season.*
In many places it is believed that if there is RAIN, SNOW, FOG, or sunshine on these days, there will be more of the same for much of the coming season. In Germany the first three days of the season are called "die drei böse Männer"—"the three evil men."

- *If robins are friendly, cold weather will come.*
- *The higher the hornets build their nests the colder the weather will be.*
- *Dogs eat grass just before rain.*
- *There will be as many freezing days in the winter as there were sunny days in the summer.*
- *Bears grow heavy coats before a cold winter.*
- *If November 11 is cold, there will be a short and mild winter.*
- *If dandelions bloom in April, July will be hot and rainy.*
- *If it rains the first Sunday in a month, it will rain every Sunday.*

- RED *sky at night,*
  Sailors' delight.
  Red sky in the morning,
  Sailors take warning.
  In parts of the world far from water, the superstition mentions shepherds.

- *Rain before seven*
  SUN *before eleven.*

- *Mackerel sky,*
  Mackerel sky,
  Never long wet,
  Never long dry.
  A "mackerel sky" is a sky full of cirrocumulus clouds—small flaky-looking clouds or clouds in small round masses arranged in groups and lines.

- Rain can be driven away by saying either of the following CHARMS:

> *Rain, rain, go away,*
> *Come again another day.*

> *Rain on the GREEN grass,*
> *Rain on a TREE,*
> *Rain on the hillside,*
> *But not on me.*

(See LIGHTNING, MOON, STORMS, THUNDER, WHIRLWIND, WIND)

Wedding band • *Harm can come to one who takes off a wedding band even for a minute.*
- *If the groom drops the wedding band during the ceremony, the marriage is doomed.*
- *To lose a wedding band is to lose love from the marriage.*
A wedding band is usually worn on the third FINGER of the LEFT hand. It was once thought that a vein in that finger went directly to the heart. The finger is really the best place to wear a RING, since a right-handed person uses that finger less than any other.
(See CIRCLE)

Wedding cake • *A BRIDE must cut her own wedding cake, helped only by the groom, or the marriage will have no sweetness.*
- *A slice of wedding cake placed under the pillow of an unmarried person will produce a dream of the future mate.*
- *A piece of wedding cake kept under the marriage bed will keep husband and wife faithful to each other.*
- *A wedding guest who does not taste the wedding cake is endangering the bride or groom.*

144

Wedding couple • *The couple being married should always stand with their feet parallel to the* CRACKS *in the floor. If they stand crossways, they are inviting evil spirits and bad luck into their marriage.*

• *If the* NUMBER *of letters of the bride and groom's first names, added together, is even, the groom will live longer than the bride. If the number is odd, the bride will live longer.*

(See BRIDE, ORANGE BLOSSOMS, PENNY, TREE, WHITE WOOL)

Wedding day • *The spouse who goes to sleep first on the wedding day will be the first to die.*

(See MARCH, MAY, JUNE*)*

Wedding dress

• *Marry in* GREEN, *ashamed to be seen.*
Marry in brown, live in town.
Marry in BLUE, *always be true.*
Marry in black, love you will lack.
Marry in white, all is right.
Marry in YELLOW, *get the wrong fellow.*
Marry in gray, a widow some day.
(See VEIL)

Wednesday • *The* SUN *shines every Wednesday, if only for a minute. If one Wednesday should pass without even a sunbeam, there will soon be a terrible storm.*

Whirlwind · *To pass through a whirlwind of dust on the road is to bring evil to your journey.*
To stop the evil, go home again. No good can come of your trip.

Whistling · Bad luck and whistling have been connected in people's minds since ancient times. Early people heard the wind whistling in trees and grass and thought the sound was the noise made by unseen spirits. When people learned how to whistle, the sound was still thought by many to be the sound of evil spirits.
- *If you whistle aboard a ship you will whistle up a storm.*
- *You should always snap your fingers when you whistle for your dog or you will whistle up the devil as well as the dog.*
- *If you whistle in a theater you will cause the play to fail.*
- *If the member of the cast of a play whistles backstage, he or she will miss a cue or fall during the play.*
- *A whistling woman is heartless.*
- *A whistling woman and a crowing hen*
  Are good for neither God nor men.

The superstitions against a whistling woman may come from an old story which tells of a woman who stood watching and whistling as the nails which were used to crucify Jesus were forged.
(See URINATION)

White heather · *White heather in the house brings bad luck.*

White horse · *A white HORSE is good luck; to own one will ensure a long life.*
White horses often live longer than dark ones and so are thought by some people to be a living AMULET against an early death.
- *It is bad luck to meet a white horse at midday or midnight.*
- *It is bad luck to meet a white horse soon after leaving home in the evening.*

Because a white horse can look ghostly at night, it was connected with evil and bad luck. To break the bad luck, SPIT on the ground and turn THREE times with the SUN. Or, spit on your right thumb and hit the palm of your LEFT hand with it to stamp out the evil.

• If you see a white horse at any other time than midday, midnight, or soon after leaving home in the evening, it is a sign that you will soon find something good. To ensure the luck, say the following charm:

> *White, white, white horse,*
> *Sing, sing, sing,*
> *On my way I'll find something.*

White rabbit • *A white rabbit is the spirit of a deceived lover.*

White wool • In Morocco, white wool is a good omen. A weaver will protect herself from evil by making a KNOT with a strand of white wool in a headdress. And a few pieces of white wool will be tied around an animal's leg to protect the animal from taking a wrong step. On a wedding day, the friends and family of a Moroccan bride may tie a bit of white wool around her FINGER; only the groom should remove this wool.

Whooping cough • To cure whooping cough, tie a hairy caterpillar, in a bag drawn tight with a RED string, around the patient's chest. As the caterpillar dies, the cough will disappear.

• Put a cup of milk on the floor and let a CAT drink half of it. Feed the other half of the milk to a patient with whooping cough. The patient will get well, but the cat will die.

• In France, and in many other parts of the world, a roasted mouse has been considered the best cure for whooping cough. (See BRAMBLE ARCH, IVY)

Widow's peak • Hair which grows down the middle of a person's forehead in a point is called a "widow's peak."
• *A widow's peak is a sign of intelligence and long life.*
• *If a woman has a widow's peak, her first husband will die young and she will soon marry again.*

Wind
• *When the wind is in the east, life is bad*
    for man and beast;
When the wind is in the north, old folks
    should not go forth;
When the wind is in the south, it blows
    the bait in the fishes' mouth;
When the wind is in the west, of all the
    winds it is the best.
• *When seabirds fly to land*
Then a windstorm is at hand.
• *No weather is ill*
If the wind be still,
But the sharper the blast
The sooner it's past.
• *Babies and old people are always irritable when the wind is in the northeast.*
(See HALLOWEEN, PALM SUNDAY)

Window • *All windows should be opened at the moment of* DEATH *so that the soul can easily leave.*
• *If a* ROBIN *flies into a room through the window, death will shortly follow.*
• *A robin tapping at the window of a sickroom is a sign that the patient will soon die.*
(See DARKNESS, MOON, NEW YEAR'S EVE)

Windowsill • *If you spill water on your windowsill you will be poor all your life.*

Wishbone • The wishbone of a bird can be used for a good luck AMULET. Often, however, it is used as a wishing CHARM. If two people pull the wishbone apart and make a wish as the bone breaks, the person with the bigger part is supposed to get the wish. Some people say and accept the meaning of the following charm while breaking the wishbone:

Shortest to marry;
Longest to tarry.

Wishes • Different peoples have wished on many things, but none are so popular as the STARS. The following CHARM, or one like it, exists in many countries:

Star light, star bright,
First star I see tonight,
I wish I may, I wish I might
Have the wish I wish tonight.

It is said that the wish will come true only if you do not look at the star again that night.

• *If you make a wish while throwing a coin in a well or a fountain, the wish will come true.*
It was once thought that spirits lived in water, especially water that was not running. Gifts were thrown to the spirits in the hope that they would keep the water pure.
• *If you make a wish at the bottom of a steep hill, and then walk up the hill without speaking or looking back, your wish will come true.*

- If two people say the same word at the same time, they can each have a wish come true by using the following charm: without speaking, link little fingers of right hands together and, taking turns (except for the last line which is said together) say,

> *Needles,*
> *Pins,*
> *Triplets,*
> *Twins.*
> *When we marry*
> *Our trouble begins.*
> *What goes up the chimney?*
> *Smoke.*
> *What comes down the chimney?*
> *Santa Claus.*
> *May your wish and my wish never be broke.*

Witches • *A witch cannot stand the presence of* IRON.
- *A witch cannot be seen in a* MIRROR.
- *All witches can say the Lord's Prayer backwards.*
- *Witches can turn themselves into any bird or animal except the* ROBIN.

- Witches have power over and use many animals. (See BLACK CAT, FOX, HORSE) AMULETS made from animals, however, can protect against witches. (See HORSESHOE, WOLF)
- *A witch can cry only* THREE *tears and those from the* LEFT *eye.*
- *If you put open* SCISSORS *under a witch's chair while the witch is seated in it, the witch cannot stand up.*
  Scissors were once made of iron.
- *To take the curse off a child who has been bewitched, stand it on its head and count ninety-nine backwards.* (See NUMBERS)
- *If you lend a witch anything, the witch will be able to control you.*
- *A witch can be killed with a bullet made on a* FRIDAY *when there is a new moon.*
- CROSS *your fingers or make a* FIG SIGN *to keep the evil away from you when you see a witch.*
  (See BLUE, BUTTON, CLOTHES, EVIL EYE, FINGER, FRIDAY THE THIRTEENTH, KNIFE)

Wolf • *If you see a wolf yawning, it is a warning to beware of empty promises.*
- *The right eye of a wolf, carried in your right hand, will protect you from witches between midnight and dawn while you are outside.*

Worms • *To cure a child or a dog of worms, take a* HAIR *from a horse's forelock and give it to the patient to eat between two pieces of buttered bread.*

Wren • *If you kill a wren or destroy its nest, you will break a bone during the coming year.*
- *The wren and the redbreast,*
  The martin and the swallow—
  Touch one of their eggs,
  Bad luck is sure to follow.

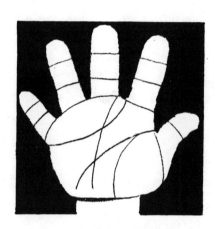

X • *The number of Xs in the palm of your right hand is the number of children you will have.*

• *If you meet a stranger on the road, you must make an X in the dirt with the toe of your* RIGHT *foot to keep yourself safe from harm.*

A stranger might turn out to be the devil, and care has to be taken to keep him from gaining control over you. (See CROSS) In some places it was thought safer to SPIT or take THREE steps backward to offset the possible evil.

• *It is bad luck to mark an X on an underground wall.*

Miners in parts of England, Germany, and the United States believe that an X on an underground wall of a mine will "mark the spot" of a future disaster.

Yawn • *A yawn is a sign that danger is near.*
To stop the danger, snap your fingers THREE times.
(See NOISE)

• *A yawn is catching.*
Because a yawn is catching, it is polite to apologize after
yawning because you have exposed another person to
danger.

• *There is only one yawn in the world, and it goes from
person to person.*

• *Cover your mouth when you yawn, or your soul can go out
of your body along with the yawn.*

• *The devil makes you yawn so that he has a chance to get
into your body.*
You can stop the devil from entering your mouth by
making the sign of the CROSS in front of your mouth as
you yawn. (See SNEEZE)

Yellow • Yellow, like GREEN, is thought by some to be
an unlucky color. The superstition started when the
devil wore yellow clothing in medieval plays. (See
WEDDING DRESS)

Youth • *You can keep your youth by eating one snake a
month at the time of the full MOON.*

Zodiac • The zodiac is an imaginary belt in the sky that is divided into twelve constellations, or STAR signs. The twelve signs correspond with twelve time divisions of the year. A person born during a particular time is said to be born under the sign for that period. The sign under which a person is born is thought to give the person special characteristics. A person born near the beginning or end of a sign may be influenced by the nearest sign. The signs of the Zodiac are often made into AMULETS and carried for good luck. Each person is supposed to carry an amulet of the sign under which he or she was born. (See BIRTHSTONE)

Aries, the Ram ♈ (*March 21 to April 19*)
Lucky day: Thursday. Unlucky day: Monday. Best months: June and July. Persons born under the sign of Aries are energetic and forceful. They are also obstinate, independent, and sometimes pushy. They are often philosophers and thinkers.

Taurus, the Bull ♉ (*April 20 to May 20*)
Lucky day: Monday. Unlucky day: Sunday. Best months: November and December. Persons born under the sign of Taurus are brave, strong, and fearless, but also kind and gentle. They are often determined and sly. They may be highly emotional and have special insights into the emotions of others.

Gemini, the Twins **69** *(May 21 to June 21)*
Lucky day: Friday. Unlucky day: Sunday. Best months:
April and August. Persons born under the sign of
Gemini are often very changeable. They are skillful with
their hands, creative, gentle, and make good teachers,
surgeons, and nurses.

Cancer, the Crab **Ⅱ** *(June 22 to July 22)*
Lucky day: Wednesday. Unlucky day: Saturday. Best
months: February and September. Persons born under
the sign of Cancer are often ambitious. They are restless
and fond of travel and should never marry early. They
have strong determination and a deep sense of purpose.

Leo, the Lion **♌** *(July 23 to August 22)*
Lucky day: Sunday. Unlucky day: Tuesday. Best
months: January and October. Persons born under the
sign of Leo are brave and dignified. They are honest,
sympathetic, and faithful. They generally have the
ability to manage things well.

Virgo, the Virgin **♍** *(August 23 to September 22)*
Lucky day: Monday. Unlucky day: Wednesday. Best
months: February and November. Persons born under
the sign of Virgo are systematic and orderly. They are
good scholars, clever, and successful in business. They
are often intolerant of ignorance.

Libra, the Balance **♎** *(September 23 to October 23)*
Lucky day: Monday. Unlucky day: Thursday. Best
months: August and December. Persons born under the
sign of Libra dislike working and are not careful in
money matters. They have a good sense of humor and
are often good-looking and graceful.

Scorpio, the Scorpion ♏ *(October 24 to November 21)*
Lucky day: Tuesday. Unlucky day: Monday. Best
months: January and July. Persons born under the sign
of Scorpio are ambitious and love praise and flattery.
They are self-controlled, practical, and sensible. They
are often capable of making fine speeches.

Sagittarius, the Archer ♐ *(November 22 to December 21)*
Lucky day: Sunday. Unlucky day: Friday. Best months:
February and June. Persons born under the sign of
Sagittarius are warmhearted and fond of children. They
are impulsive, but honest. They are often good at sports.

Capricorn, the Goat ♑ *(December 22 to January 19)*
Lucky day: Wednesday. Unlucky day: Saturday. Best
months: March and November. Persons born under the
sign of Capricorn are often fond of music. Economical
and careful, they are hard workers who usually are good
in business. They are generally sympathetic and
considerate of others.

Aquarius, the Water Bearer ♒ *(January 20 to February 18)*
Lucky day: Thursday. Unlucky day: Wednesday. Best
months: April and August. Persons born under the sign
of Aquarius often put things off. They are pleasant and
generally agreeable, seldom ill tempered. They are often
restless and not fond of work.

Pisces, the Fish ♓ *(February 19 to March 20)*
Lucky day: Wednesday. Unlucky day: Friday. Best
months: May and November. Persons born under the
sign of Pisces are born for love. They are creative,
sensitive, generous, and fond of art and nature. Often
they are also fickle and easily led.

If you would like to read
more about superstitions . . .

Julie Forsyth Batchelor and Claudia de Lys. **Superstition? Here's Why!**
Illustrated by Erik Blegvad. Voyager: New York, 1954. (Paper)
A light treatment of the reasons behind some of today's most common
superstitions.

R. Brasch. **How Did It Begin?** David McKay Company: New York, 1967.
An exploration of the customs and superstitions, rooted in the fears of
ancient and primitive peoples, which still guide our daily activities.

Encyclopedia Judaica. Macmillan: New York, 1971.
A very interesting article on amulets traces their use, by Jews and Christians,
through history. Special emphasis is placed on the Middle Ages. Fascinating
illustrations of old amulets. The volumes of the encyclopedia are available
in many large libraries.

Arthur S. Gregor. **Amulets, Talismans, and Fetishes.** Illustrated by Anne
Burgess. Charles Scribner's Sons: New York, 1975.
A discussion of the historical and present use of amulets, talismans, and
fetishes. Complete with a dictionary of amulets, charms, remedies, brews
and spells.

Marcia Leach. **The Soup Stone.** Decorations by Mamie Harmon. Funk &
Wagnalls Company: New York, 1954.
The stories behind superstitions about everyday items—shoes, salt, needles,
pins, mirrors, and teen-agers.

Lillian Morrison. **Touch Blue.** Thomas Y. Crowell Company: New York, 1958.
Some common and some not-so-common charms and rhymes explained in
terms of the historical period in which they originated. A sort of "inside"
Mother Goose.

Vance Randolph. **Ozark Superstitions.** Dover Publications: New York,
1964. (Paper)
A classic collection of superstitions gathered in the early part of the century
from people living in the hidden valleys and remote peaks of the Ozark
Mountains. To many of the people interviewed, the superstitions were not
curious sayings, but rules to live by.

Alvin Schwartz. **Cross Your Fingers, Spit in Your Hat: Superstitions and
Other Beliefs.** Illustrated by Glen Rounds. J. B. Lippincott Company:
Philadelphia, 1974. (Paper)
Superstitions about everything from ailments to warts—some traditional,
some remembered from the author's childhood, others collected from
school children, friends, and folklorists. Made even more special by terrific
illustrations.

Joshua Trachtenberg. **Jewish Magic and Superstition: A Study in Folk Religion.** Atheneum: New York, 1970.
A discussion of the reasons for, and the purposes and methods of, magic and superstition within a religion. A serious work, but easy to understand and absolutely fascinating.

Eliot Wigginton, Ed. **The Foxfire Book.** Anchor Books: New York, 1972. (Paper)
Life in the Appalachian Mountains as told by some older residents to junior and senior high school students who turned the talk into a book. Includes planting by signs of the moon, faith healing, snake lore, mountain crafts, and food.